TPM FOR WORKSHOP LEADERS

TPM FOR
WORKSHOP LEADERS

Kunio Shirose

Publisher's Message by
Norman Bodek

Productivity Press
Portland, Oregon

Originally published as *Gemba leader notameno TPM* © 1984 by the Japan Institute of Plant Maintenance, Japan.

English edition © 1992 by Productivity Press, Inc. Translated by Bruce Talbot.

Productivity Press
P.O. Box 13390
Portland, OR 97213-0390
Telephone: (503) 235-0600
Telefax: (503) 235-0909

Cover design by Joyce C. Weston
Printed and bound by Maple-Vail Book Manufacturing Group
Printed in the United States of America

Library of Congress Cataloging-in-Publication Data

Shirose, Kunio.
  [Gemba leader notameno TPM. English]
  TPM for workshop leaders / Kunio Shirose.
    p. cm.
  Translation of: Gemba riida no tameno TPM.
  ISBN 0-915299-92-5
  1. Plant maintenance—Management. I. Title.
TS192.S55 1992
  658.2—dc20   91-26611
                                    CIP

99 98 97 96 95   10 9 8 7 6 5 4

Contents

NOTE: Due to the format requirements of the illustrations, some of which are two-page spreads, you will occasionally find a blank page. Please note that these are intentional, and that there is no material missing from the book.

Preface

TPM — total productive maintenance — has gained widespread attention in recent years. It has become a hot topic for many reasons, such as its concrete results: TPM not only prevents breakdowns but also reduces defects, idling, minor stoppages, and other problems. The result is much more efficient equipment.

TPM also solves problems conventional management methods cannot; that is, it reduces chronic defects and eliminates the need for fine-tuning. In addition, it provides a method for monitoring equipment deterioration. Over the years equipment gets dirty, develops leaks, and gathers cutting debris, so without a method of monitoring this deterioration, it becomes easier and easier to overlook abnormalities.

Companies that thoroughly implement TPM aim for "zero breakdowns" and "zero defects." It is not unusual for them to succeed in reducing breakdowns to about 1/100th and defects to about 1/40th of their pre-TPM levels.

Every company that adopts the TPM approach must accept three imperatives:

- The quality and functioning of the equipment must change.
- The equipment operators must change their way of thinking about the equipment.
- As a result, the workplace itself must change dramatically.

In my capacity as a consultant at JIPM (Japan Institute for Plant Maintenance) I have spent many years promoting the development and spread of TPM. One of the fruits of my labor as a TPM consultant was the book *TPM Development Program*, which I coauthored with several other TPM consultants. Building on that foundation, I wrote this book to help the leaders of manufacturing workshops understand the TPM approach. These leaders are hereafter referred to simply as "workshop leaders." Naturally, this book can also be recommended to maintenance department leaders.

I also intended this book to form part of a series that began with Seiichi Nakajima's *Introduction to TPM*, which was aimed primarily at managers of manufacturing companies. The reader is advised to read Mr. Nakajima's book as well.

For this book, I have selected several case studies from my own experience as a TPM leader. As a result, it may be a little subjective in parts, but my original intention was to pass along the improvement philosophy I have developed through many years of experience. Due to my extensive experience in leading improvements in mechanical assembly operations I frequently focus on machine industries; therefore some parts of the book may not be very well suited to readers from the process industry. However, I would encourage the reader to pay particular attention to the sections that discuss the goals of TPM, P-M analysis, and autonomous maintenance, as well as the philosophy and approach to reducing chronic losses.

In one part, I stress the concept of "slight defects" when I discuss a certain approach to making improvements. It was Mr. Masakatsu Nakaigawa, the inventor of "skill management," who taught me the importance of slight defects as a key contribution to productivity loss, and I would like to thank him here for his ideas, which I am passing along in this book.

I would also like to thank the people at Kubota Steel's plastics factory, Topy Industries, Daihatsu Motor Co., Nachi-Fujikoshi Corp., Bando Chemical Industries, and Matsushita Electric for their kind and generous cooperation in efforts to develop TPM. Thanks also to the people at Nachi-Fujikoshi and Daihatsu who have provided various reference materials.

Finally, I wish to thank the people at JIPM who provided indispensable assistance: Messrs. Nakajima, Suzuki, Miyoshi, and Gotoh, as well as the chief editor, Mr. Soneda, for his expert advice regarding compilation and publication tasks.

Kunio Shirose
Executive Vice President
Assistant Director of TPM Operations Division
Japan Institute for Plant Maintenance
October 1984

Publisher's Message

To remain competitive in today's global marketplace, a manufacturing company needs a cost-effective system designed to maintain peak operation of production machinery. Total productive maintenance (TPM) is rapidly becoming the system of choice. The author of this book, *TPM for Workshop Leaders*, spent many years promoting TPM in his role as consultant at the Japan Institute for Plant Maintenance (JIPM). He was also a contributing author to the book *TPM Development Program* published by Productivity Press in 1989.

TPM can form the foundation for improvements to the entire production process, and the author defines it as "a set of activities for restoring equipment to its optimal conditions and changing the work environment to maintain those conditions." This definition of TPM is deceptively simple. Maintaining optimal equipment conditions means more than just making sure each machine runs well — it means ensuring that it runs so well that it never breaks down; always operates at designed speed or faster with no idling or minor stoppages; never produces a defective product; and causes a minimum of startup, setup, and adjustment losses. Besides this, it means establishing and maintaining standardized methods for equipment diagnosis, early detection of abnormalities, spare parts management, parts replacement procedures, and information systems to record equipment histories and breakdown data. An effective TPM program also aims at minimizing the impact of equipment deterioration, and establishing a method to help design engineers incorporate improvements into new equipment.

It is not a simple maintenance program. TPM aims for absolutes and cannot be implemented by a handful of people. It requires the cooperation and involvement of all levels of the company, the breaking down of traditional attitudes toward specialization, and the establishment of educational systems designed to upgrade skill levels of maintenance and production personnel.

In a company implementing TPM, the factory floor workers are divided into groups or teams, each with a leader responsible for the activities of that team as they learn to care for their equipment and perform various maintenance tasks. This book deals with the practical, everyday issues that are most likely to be encountered by team leaders in both the production and maintenance departments. It provides an excellent overview of the philosophy of TPM, and describes activities for each step toward optimizing equipment efficiency and establishing an autonomous maintenance system.

Forthcoming from Productivity Press are several books that discuss some key points of a TPM program. The next book in this series describes an effective method for the reduction of minor stoppages on automated lines. Another book describes a system that integrates Quality Control (QC) with TPM and explains how these two systems can provide a foundation for effective just-in-time production.

TPM for Workshop Leaders was originally published by the Japan Institute for Plant Maintenance. For making this book accessible for an English-speaking audience, our thanks go to

Bruce Talbot for providing an excellent translation; Bruce Graham for editorial development of the text and for redrawing the characters in the cartoons created by Keijirō Kaitō ; Chris Thornton, copyediting; and Jennifer Cross, proofreading. Finally, thanks to Joyce C. Weston who designed the cover, and David Lennon, who managed the production of the book with the assistance of the production team: Gayle Joyce, Susan Cobb, Michele Saar, and Lea Simon.

Norman Bodek
Publisher

1

Causes of Breakdowns and Defects

Chronic breakdowns and defects have many causes, one of which is people, as the following example illustrates.

A worker reports to the group leader that an equipment breakdown has stopped production. Although the leader is very concerned about meeting delivery schedules and is understandably upset by the frequency of this type of breakdown, the production line obviously had to be stopped to deal with the problem. A maintenance worker is called in, and after some troubleshooting, reports the damage is serious enough to warrant replacing certain parts. However, there is some uncertainty about their availability, and downtime could be as much as four or five hours, especially if the parts had to be fabricated.

As a temporary measure, the leader decides to shift production to another machine while the repairs are being made. At this point, the maintenance worker says, "You know, this breakdown didn't happen just out of the blue. I'll bet this machine's been acting funny for at least two or three days, and this part was probably vibrating or making a strange sound. You guys should have told me about this sooner. I could have fixed it in about ten minutes during your lunch break. Please let me know as soon as you notice anything strange about *any* of these machines, OK?"

The leader agreed, but added it was obviously the responsibility of the maintenance department to teach the operators how to recognize the early signs of these problems. This seemed like a good idea, so they decided to set a meeting time.

After thinking a moment, the leader realized this was not a long-term solution and said, "But why does this kind of breakdown happen? Sometimes there are certain parts that are *always* breaking and other times, like today, some other part suddenly breaks. We don't know if it's because we're using the equipment wrong, or if the equipment itself is bad, or if the maintenance procedures are no good. Whatever the cause, it sure fouls up our work!"

Believe it or not, there is nothing unusual about the situation just described. In fact, most workplaces suffer from this same dilemma. Breakdowns are the root of all problems, because when they occur, production stops, deliveries are delayed, and product defects are created; in other words, a single breakdown can wreak havoc throughout the factory and can "break down" the entire operation. That is why you must always seek to prevent them.

In this situation, the damaged equipment had been signaling its abnormal condition through unusual vibrations or noises. If the workers had read these signs and responded promptly, the breakdown could have been avoided; so the human factor *was* the root cause of the breakdown.

As a matter of fact, whenever you look deeply enough into the reasons for *any* breakdown, you invariably find people-related causes. So if people are ultimately responsible for creating breakdowns, why shouldn't they also be able to prevent them, creating a "zero breakdown" workshop? There are ways to reduce and even completely eliminate breakdowns, and one is the subject of this book: TPM (total productive maintenance).

A detailed definition will be provided later. For now, understand it as something practiced cooperatively by two groups of people: the maintenance staff, who act as "equipment doctors," and the production staff, who work with the equipment every day.

In particular, the equipment operators need to be taught how to discover abnormalities so they can identify problems early on. For their part, the maintenance staff must apply their specialized skills to analyze equipment data provided by the production department, find the causes of breakdowns and abnormalities, and take effective measures to prevent the recurrence of similar problems.

The road to achieving zero breakdowns starts with daily equipment checks and other maintenance activities performed by the equipment operators themselves, as well as specialized activities performed by maintenance workers.

Here is another example of a workplace situation:

> One day a group leader notices the equipment operators are doing a lot more rework than usual. When asked why, one operator replies that nothing has changed in their procedures, but when they use certain material lots, the percentage of pieces needing rework seems to increase from the norm of 2 or 3 percent to 5 or 6 percent. The operator believes the problem is with the material lot.
>
> The group leader agrees that things always *do* seem to change for better or for worse each time a retooling is performed but also suspects problems with the equipment. So, of course, there are questions about what repair measures had been taken in the last week to try to correct the problem. The operator describes how a new grinding wheel, installed two days ago, did seem to correct it, but only temporarily. Then they increased the processing speed and did an extra careful job of retooling, during which all the changeover parts were precisely measured, but they *still* found the machine problematic.
>
> After a moment's thought, the group leader suggested the grinder spindle might be wobbling too much and that

the operator should look into that. A check revealed that, indeed, this was the case. So the leader was satisfied they had found the cause and told the operator to have a maintenance person repair the spindle the very next day.

In this situation, the operator was constantly having to make repair adjustments, and each one was successful for only a short time.

Why were these repairs so unsuccessful? Because they each addressed a different cause, and there were several causes for the malfunction.

For example, the precision of equipment can be measured in three different ways — static precision, dynamic precision, and jig precision. Problems can be caused by one type of imprecision or a combination. Whatever the cause, the operator or maintenance worker must respond with reworking.

These types of problems are likely to occur in any workplace, and when they do, they can lead to major production problems. What can be done to prevent them? To escape from the vicious cycle of problems and their causes, make a thorough study of *all* imaginable causes and then carry out an equally thorough set of responses.

The preceding example showed how making single repairs here and there does not reduce chronic defects. The only way to get rid of chronic defects once and for all is to be systematic and to prepare a list of all the probable causes, then do whatever is necessary to eliminate every single cause, no matter how minor.

It is not easy to understand the importance of this systematic and thorough approach; therefore this topic is discussed in more detail in Chapter 6.

THE WORKSHOP ENVIRONMENT

What conditions *promote* breakdowns and defects in typical workshop environments? To answer this, it is necessary to study overall workshop conditions in the belief that whatever these may be, they are symptomatic of the basic attitudes of the people who *use* the workshop. As you read the following lists, consider which conditions exist in your own workplace.

Condition of Equipment

- The equipment is generally very dirty.
- Cutting debris is scattered on and around the equipment.
- The equipment leaks hydraulic fluid and lubricants.
- Cutting oil is scattered around.
- Oil pans are overflowing.
- People don't mind seeing dirt and grime piling up everywhere: they think it's normal.
- Grime from the cutters and grinders is caked onto the equipment.
- Motors are coated with a layer of oil mist.
- Motors are allowed to get very hot, or they often make strange noises.
- The limit switches on the cutters and grinders are covered with oil.
- Large covers are sometimes used to protect certain machines, but their internal parts are not cleaned.
- A broken V-belt is not replaced on a machine that uses three belts. Instead, the machine is allowed to operate with only two belts.
- Some parts rattle and vibrate.
- The equipment is positioned to make access for routine maintenance checks difficult.
- Oil cans are left empty and dirty.
- Drains are clogged.
- Wires and pipes are left in chaotic configurations, making it hard to see which one goes where.

Condition of Area around Equipment

- It takes a lot of time to recover cutting debris.
- The cutting debris is scattered around so it takes a long time to sweep up.
- There is no stand for the oil cans (and the oil equipment is left dirty).
- The floor is left dirty and, in spots, slippery with oil.
- The jigs are not kept tidy and organized.
- There are a lot of useless items lying around.
- Things are not kept in specified places.

Equipment Operators

- Operators occasionally make errors.
- Operators do not perform regular equipment checks. In fact, they do not even know *how*.
- When equipment must be oiled, only some operators know when and where to oil, and how much to use. Even those who know the oiling schedule and procedure do not always perform it correctly.
- Operators do not know how to replace equipment parts or perform precision checks.
- When operators find an equipment abnormality, they call a maintenance worker without trying to figure out what is wrong themselves.
- Operators do not regard breakdowns and defects as their own problems.
- Operators use measurement instruments that have exceeded their use period.

General Conditions

- Equipment breakdowns occur frequently, at a rate of 3 percent or higher.

- It takes a long time to fix minor problems, and often the repair is only temporary.
- Repairs generally take a long time.
- Problems following changeover occur more (or less) often, depending on who does the changeover.
- Changeover and adjustments take a lot of time, and people accept adjustments as natural.
- Idling and minor stoppages happen often; extra workers handle them, but they still prevent automated processes from operating for long periods of time without human assistance.
- The C_p (process capability index) fluctuates, but its value is less than 1 (i.e., not good).
- Reworking occurs at a rate of 3 percent and has become chronic.
- It is very hard to understand the causes of problems that make rework necessary.
- The processing speed has been decreased because too many defects occurred when it was maintained at the rated speed.
- Model-specific standard cycle times have not been established.
- Workers know what the model-specific standard cycle times are but do not keep to them.
- No one has quantitatively analyzed speed loss.

If any of the preceding conditions exist in *your* workshop, it is high time to implement TPM. If done correctly, TPM will get rid of these conditions and ensure high productivity and quality. Companies that get fully behind TPM will undoubtedly get good results. There are many, many examples. However, like the building of Rome, TPM cannot be fully implemented in a day. As implied by the *total* in total productive maintenance, effective TPM requires the participation of everyone — from management to factory-floor workers.

TPM SUCCESS STORIES

Figure 1-1 shows just some of the benefits derived by companies that implemented TPM, but they are typical of its results.

Any company that implements TPM should expect to reduce its breakdowns to anywhere from 1/30 to 1/100 of their current level, and defects from 1/30 to 1/40, or more. This results in a corresponding 30 to 100 percent increase in productivity.

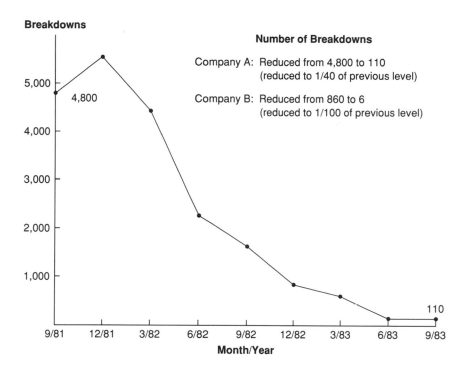

Breakdowns

Number of Breakdowns

Company A: Reduced from 4,800 to 110
(reduced to 1/40 of previous level)

Company B: Reduced from 860 to 6
(reduced to 1/100 of previous level)

4,800

110

Month/Year

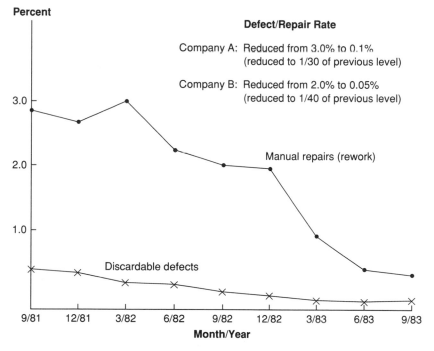

Percent

Defect/Repair Rate

Company A: Reduced from 3.0% to 0.1%
(reduced to 1/30 of previous level)

Company B: Reduced from 2.0% to 0.05%
(reduced to 1/40 of previous level)

Manual repairs (rework)

Discardable defects

Month/Year

Figure 1-1. TPM Success Statistics

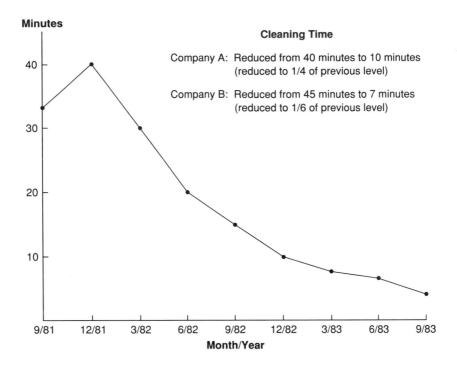

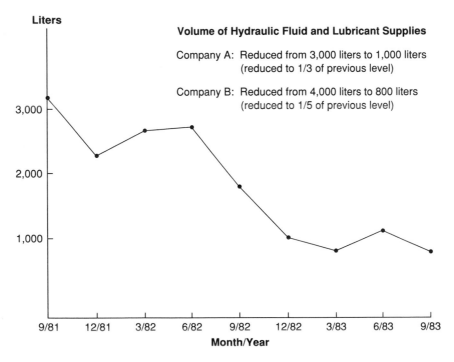

Figure 1-1. TPM Success Statistics (cont.)

2
Definition of TPM

This chapter presents a definition of TPM and explains its elements. But first, here is a brief look at the history of equipment management in Japan.

HISTORY OF EQUIPMENT MANAGEMENT IN JAPAN

What is meant by the term *equipment management*? It is the set of activities that prevents quality defects and breakdowns, eliminates the need for equipment adjustments, and makes the work easier and safer for equipment operators. The concept of PM (preventive maintenance) was introduced to Japan from the United States in 1951. Before PM, companies generally practiced BM (breakdown maintenance), which means fixing equipment only after it has broken down. The Japanese companies that adopted the American concept of preventive maintenance substantially reduced equipment breakdowns.

However, over the years the PM approach was gradually changed to meet the new demands placed on industry in the modern world. One such change was the introduction of the concept of CM (corrective maintenance), which goes beyond the restorative type of repairs performed as part of preventive maintenance. CM promotes repairs that make the same breakdown less likely to happen again. Another change came with the concept of MP (maintenance prevention), which incorporates the equipment design stage in an effort to build better equipment that is easier to maintain.

Finally, the PM, CM, and MP approaches were consolidated under a new type of approach called PM, which in this case stands for productive maintenance. *Maintenance* basically means the activities required to maintain certain conditions. If these consist of the overall optimal conditions for production, including quality, yield, and safety, then PM (productive maintenance) is required to maintain them. This is because PM is aimed toward maximizing productivity — which means profitability. To achieve this goal, PM includes four types of activities:

- Preventive maintenance
- Post-facto maintenance
- Improvement-related maintenance
- Maintenance prevention

Three of these are especially important: preventive maintenance, improvement-related maintenance, and maintenance prevention.

Preventive Maintenance

Preventive maintenance is aimed at the prevention of breakdowns and defects. Daily activities include equipment checks, precision measurements, partial or complete overhauls at specified periods, oil changes, lubrication, and so on. In addition, workers record equipment deterioration so they know to replace or repair worn parts before they cause problems.

Recent technological advances in tools for inspection and diagnosis have enabled even more accurate and reliable equipment maintenance. The term *predictive maintenance* is used to describe activities that employ these advanced technologies.

Improvement-Related Maintenance

Improvement-related maintenance activities are those intended to improve the equipment, and thereby reduce future breakdowns or defects. In addition, they make the equipment easier to maintain.

In other words, once you understand its weak points, make improvements designed to eliminate them. This, in turn, will facilitate checking, oiling, parts replacement and changeover, as well as the other activities equipment operators carry out from day to day.

Maintenance Prevention

In the development of new equipment, maintenance prevention is needed at the design stage. These activities are aimed at making the equipment reliable, easy to take care of, and user-friendly so operators can easily retool, adjust, and otherwise operate it.

TPM: JAPANESE-STYLE EQUIPMENT MANAGEMENT

Equipment management in Japan has evolved from preventive to productive maintenance, and it should be recognized this management style was introduced to Japan largely from the United States.

However, American-style equipment management was characterized by activities performed by the maintenance department. As such, it was never very successful at achieving zero breakdowns or zero defects. That is where Japanese-style PM comes in. TPM is Japan's answer to American-style PM.

Based on small-group activities, TPM takes PM companywide, gaining the support and cooperation of everyone from top management down. It goes beyond the maintenance department to involve the whole company, and that is how PM (preventive maintenance) became TPM (total productive maintenance).

After all, the people most likely to first notice equipment abnormalities or other strange symptoms are not the maintenance staff but the operators who work with the equipment day in and day out. So the best way to prevent breakdowns is to have the operators give prompt notice of abnormalities and then have the maintenance staff promptly respond with corrective measures. Obviously, this cannot be done without active cooperation of equipment operators.

TPM, therefore, is characterized by production department workers participating in maintenance activities.

DEFINITION OF TPM

A full definition of TPM contains the following five points (see Figure 2-1):

1. It aims at getting the most efficient use of equipment (i.e., overall efficiency).
2. It establishes a total (companywide) PM system encompassing maintenance prevention, preventive maintenance, and improvement-related maintenance.
3. It requires the participation of equipment designers, equipment operators, and maintenance department workers.
4. It involves every employee from top management down.
5. It promotes and implements PM based on autonomous, small-group activities.

Bringing the whole company together behind TPM enables it to actually achieve goals such as zero breakdowns and zero defects, and these pay off in higher productivity and enhanced profitability.

Figure 2-1. Definition of TPM

THE FIVE PILLARS OF TPM DEVELOPMENT

The following is a brief description of what are called the five pillars of TPM development:

1. Implement improvement activities designed to increase equipment efficiency. This is accomplished mainly by eliminating the "six big losses." (These will be explained later.)

2. Establish a system of autonomous maintenance to be performed by equipment operators. This is set up after they are trained to be "equipment-conscious" and "equipment-skilled."

3. Establish a planned maintenance system. This increases the efficiency of the maintenance department.

4. Establish training courses. These help equipment operators raise their skill levels.

5. Establish a system for MP design and early equipment management. MP design generates equipment that requires less maintenance, while early equipment management gets new equipment operating normally in less time.

While all five pillars are essential to TPM development, most important for workshop leaders are the first three. Accordingly, these will be described in a separate chapter of this book.

Figure 2-2 presents an overview of TPM. The elements summarized will be explained in more detail in subsequent chapters, but for now Figure 2-2 provides an overall picture of TPM. It might also prove useful as a review summary to use after reading this book.

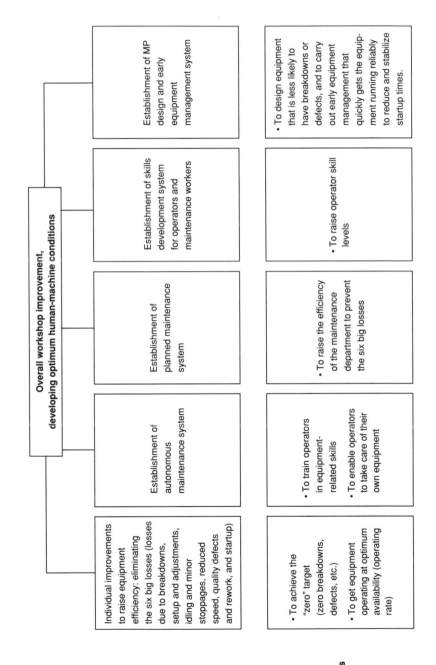

Overall workshop improvement, developing optimum human-machine conditions

Individual improvements to raise equipment efficiency: eliminating the six big losses (losses due to breakdowns, setup and adjustments, idling and minor stoppages, reduced speed, quality defects and rework, and startup)

Establishment of autonomous maintenance system

Establishment of planned maintenance system

Establishment of skills development system for operators and maintenance workers

Establishment of MP design and early equipment management system

Goals

• To achieve the "zero" target (zero breakdowns, defects, etc.)

• To get equipment operating at optimum availability (operating rate)

• To train operators in equipment-related skills

• To enable operators to take care of their own equipment

• To raise the efficiency of the maintenance department to prevent the six big losses

• To raise operator skill levels

• To design equipment that is less likely to have breakdowns or defects, and to carry out early equipment management that quickly gets the equipment running reliably to reduce and stabilize startup times.

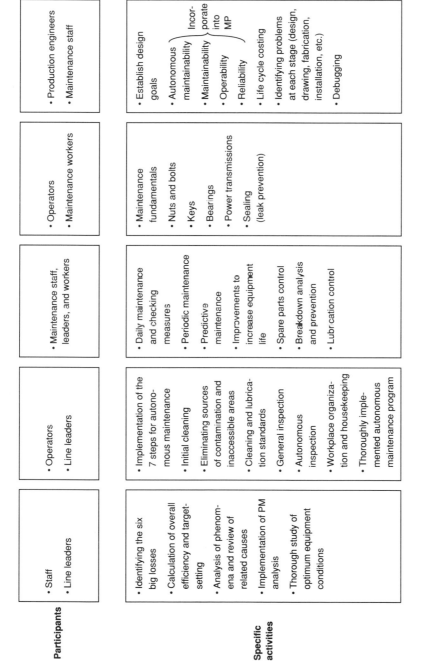

Figure 2-2. TPM Overview

3

Characteristics and Goals

of TPM

TPM IS CHARACTERIZED BY "ZERO" TARGETS

One of the main characteristics of TPM is its aggressive pursuit of absolute goals, such as zero breakdowns and zero defects. In order to have "zero" anything, it must be prevented from happening even once. Therefore TPM emphasizes prevention above all else, and this means taking preventive action. It is simply too late if you wait for a problem to happen and then fix it. In TPM, prevention is based on the following three principles:

1. Maintenance of Normal Conditions. To maintain normal operating conditions, operators must prevent deterioration by cleaning, checking, oiling, tightening, and precision-checking the equipment on a daily basis.

2. Early Discovery of Abnormalities. While performing these activities, operators must use their senses and measurement tools to detect abnormalities as soon as they appear. Maintenance workers should also conduct periodic diagnostic tests to check for abnormalities using specialized tools.

3. Prompt Response. Operators and maintenance staff cannot afford to delay responses to abnormalities.

TWO MAIN GOALS OF TPM

The two main goals of TPM are to develop optimal conditions for the workshop as a human-machine system and to improve the overall quality of the workplace.

Development of Optimal Conditions for the Workshop as a Human-Machine System

Every workshop consists of a particular combination of two components: people (operators) and machines (equipment). No matter how these are combined — one operator per machine, one operator handling several machines, or a control board for automated machines, transfer machines, or robots — the workshop system consists of people working closely with machines. We call these *human-machine systems.*

How efficiently each human-machine system functions to manufacture products depends mainly on how well human work meshes with the work of machines. Human work includes operating the machines correctly, blade retooling, adjusting, cleaning, oiling, replacing parts, etc., while machine work can include things like maintaining standard motions, precision, tolerances, etc.

The role of equipment operators also involves checking how well the functions of the equipment are being used and applying the results to get better use of it. While it is the equipment that actually makes the products, the operators and maintenance staff have the major responsibility of maintaining its health. To get maximum use of equipment, the ideal condition of each component must be known, as well as the measurement values that indicate peak performance. Once these conditions and values are known, the job is to maintain them. The more complicated the equipment is, the greater human responsibility becomes.

Unfortunately, very few workshops come even remotely close to understanding and maintaining ideal conditions. Most have an awkward combination of people and machines, and a walk around practically any workshop will show equipment no longer in top shape. Perhaps it was once in good shape, but people have let it deteriorate. They do not adequately keep spindle vibrations within range, maintain standard measurement methods, carry out periodic measurements, or set dynamic precision standards. It is no wonder that such workshops have frequent equipment problems requiring disruptive and time-consuming repairs. Since most operators are not skilled in detecting equipment abnormalities, often they do not notice when equipment is giving signs of trouble, and they take it for granted they must deal with problems only as they arise.

Such a state of affairs exists in most workplaces because operators leave the major production role to the machines and limit their own to operating equipment and checking the quality of the products. They are not concerned with acquiring the ability to detect abnormalities. The maintenance workers view their role as simply repairing sporadic breakdowns. They couldn't care less about defect loss, reduced speed loss, or other losses incurred by equipment operating in less-than-ideal condition. As long as it runs fairly well, they are satisfied.

Never forget: the main role in every human-machine system is the human one.

Finding the Best Combination of Roles

Developing optimal conditions for the workshop as a human-machine system means finding the best combination of human and machine conditions.

For the machine side, that means getting the equipment into shape to prevent the six big losses and establishing its optimal availability. To do this, you must methodically identify and solve each problem that arises, both sporadic and chronic ones, by applying the improvement approach described in Chapter 6, and gaining the active participation of operators, maintenance staff, and production engineers.

There are two main points to remember about establishing an optimal human-machine system:

- Restore equipment to optimal operating conditions. This requires thoroughly researching the ideal conditions for each group of parts or equipment units.
- Keep the equipment running at optimal operating conditions. In this regard, the particular responsibilities of operators, maintenance workers, and other technical staff must be thoroughly defined and carried out.

In summary, one of the two main goals of TPM is to establish a clear understanding of the roles of people and machines in the workshop and to ensure they are performed correctly to create an optimal human-machine system.

Improving the Overall Quality of the Workplace

It is hardly an exaggeration to say that most workplaces are awash in loss, mainly due to a preponderance of quality defects and breakdowns. And no matter how hard workers strive to turn out good products, they always end up dealing with lots of defects and rework. Why do these losses occur? The reason is simple: because no one has done anything to change the workplace conditions that *cause* them. In other words, nothing can prevent quality defects and rework until the workplace itself is changed.

Changing the Way of Seeing and Thinking about Things

To change the workplace, there must be a change in the way of thinking about it and everything in it. With current attitudes, there is no recognition of the abnormalities and defects that exist in the machines, jigs, and tools that are used. For example, when a jig starts wearing down or vibrating, most operators either do not notice it or do not feel the need to do anything about it. But this must change. Operators need to concern themselves with even these minor defects, because the overall quality of the workplace, good or bad, is entirely the result of human behavior. So the most important thing for workers to cultivate is an ability to discover even the most minor abnormalities *before* they develop into major problems.

Seeing Each Breakdown and Defect as an Embarrassment

It is all too easy to find workshops where the operators look at breakdowns, quality defects, and rework as someone else's fault: blame is usually put on the maintenance staff and/or production engineers. This is a big problem. Quality improvement will not go anywhere until equipment operators and other workers take responsibility for their workplace, regarding every breakdown or defect as an embarrassment. Whenever they occur, the operators should seriously consider how they let such a thing happen.

Taking responsibility also means taking action. When a breakdown occurs, the operator concerned should meet with a maintenance worker to find out exactly what he or she did that caused it or could have done to prevent it. Then the operator can figure out a way to keep the same thing from happening again. All this should be done on the initiative of the operator.

Once workers take personal responsibility, as they clean and check equipment, they will bring new concern and attention to their work. Gradually, the workplace will improve.

TPM strongly emphasizes quality-consciousness among operators and improvement of the overall quality of the workplace. Still, attitudes are not easily changed. Changing the equipment, the people, and the entire workplace has to proceed step by step.

Equipment must be changed so it is sparkling clean and will not develop abnormalities so easily, and the workplace must be changed so its overall quality is improved (see Figure 3-1). People, on the other hand, must change *themselves* so they understand and treat their work — and workshop — in a new and better way.

Some of these points deserve more detailed discussion.

Changing the Equipment

In TPM, to change the equipment, go through the following steps:

- Cleaning becomes checking.
- Checking becomes discovery of abnormalities.
- Abnormalities become things to be restored or improved.
- Restoration and improvement become positive effects.
- Positive effects become pride in the workplace.

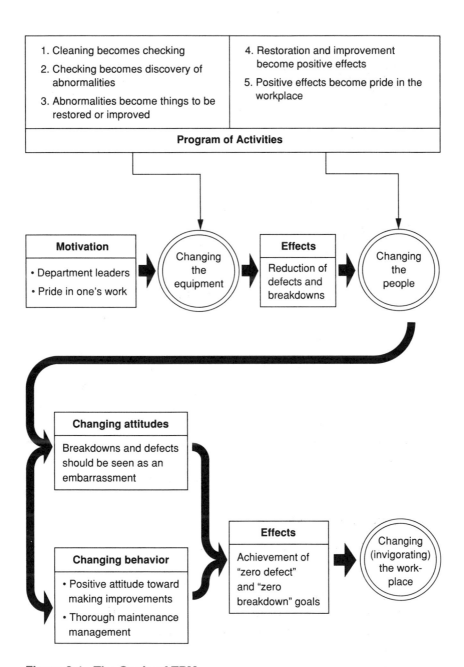

Figure 3-1. The Goals of TPM

Put another way, when you learn to discover abnormalities, you begin to create a workshop free of abnormalities and can then begin to enjoy it. The pleasure of making improvements is the basic motivator for changing equipment and human behavior.

Here is a closer look at each of these steps.

Cleaning becomes checking; checking becomes discovery of abnormalities. Cleaning equipment requires you to touch and move it, coming into closer contact with it, making it easier to tell when it is acting abnormally. That is why "cleaning becomes checking." In fact, cleaning a machine is one of the best ways to check for abnormalities. For example, while cleaning a machine component, you may notice something loose inside. Then you may wonder how it got that way — through normal wear or perhaps because of a buildup of dust or other contaminants. You may also wonder what might happen if the part is left as it is.

When cleaning becomes checking, checking in turn becomes a means of discovering abnormalities and dealing with them at an early stage. Here is a case that illustrates this point.

> One workshop began its improvement efforts with a thorough cleaning, during which everyone's face, hands, and clothes turned black with dust and grime. At first the workers were very reluctant to do the cleaning; they made complaints, such as "What's the point of getting all this stuff so clean? It's just going to get dirty again! It's a waste of time! We'd be smarter if we just got the equipment working better to increase the output. We're not here to clean, you know."
>
> However, when the cleaning got under way, the workers were surprised to discover how much could be learned by coming into contact with every part of the machines. They found strange things they never suspected to exist and looked into areas that had always been closed up and invisible. In no time, they prepared a long list of suspected abnormalities.

As this shows, when operators learn how to discover abnormalities and practice it, often with the help of maintenance staff, they eventually learn to see their equipment in a whole new way. They learn to use all their senses to better understand the equipment and its condition. When workers carry out an initial cleaning, it is not unusual for them to find anywhere from 10 to 50 abnormalities in each machine!

Abnormalities become things to be restored or improved. The next step is to once again get your hands dirty in an effort to better understand the abnormalities that were discovered and come up with ways of restoring or improving them. You can easily repair some defective components, while others can or must be replaced. Perhaps the wiring layout needs better organization or a loose part needs tightening. Study the problems and try solutions.

Often this is much easier said than done. It may be difficult, especially at first, to figure out just what the problem is or how to solve it. But it is only by struggling with puzzling problems and finding difficult solutions that equipment operators come to appreciate the issues with which maintenance workers must deal. This experience also helps operators learn they cannot be nonchalant and allow troublesome problems to happen again.

Consider an oil pan that is dirty soon after it was cleaned. Realizing how much trouble keeping the oil pan clean will be, the operator wonders what could be dirtying it so quickly. A close look at the fluid reveals a combination of cutting oil, hydraulic oil, and lubricant. The operator locates these leakage points and realizes an improvement must be devised. After laboriously trying various solutions, the operator finally devises a set of improvements that stop the leaks. Having worked so hard, this worker is naturally concerned about taking preventive action to avoid dealing with the same problem again.

Restoration and improvement become positive effects. Things that are restored or improved rarely remain that way on their own. Often, they start deteriorating sooner than expected and in no time are back to their former condition. But this is no reason to give up. When an improvement does not last, it's time to start thinking of ways to maintain it, perhaps by using a different approach. When someone has followed a hard-won, successful improvement with a hard-won search for ways to maintain that improvement, he or she can be doubly proud. As the saying goes, the bigger the battle, the greater the glory. This sense of achievement then becomes the impetus for further improvements.

From the viewpoint of the operator, the process of "changing the equipment" involves cultivating a sharp eye for abnormalities, taking the trouble to fix them, and experiencing the pleasure of making successful improvements and finding ways to maintain them. Even a machine that seems no better than a rickety old junk heap can be cleaned and improved until it runs like a Swiss watch.

There is no joy or glory in going halfway; it takes determination to change equipment the TPM way.

Changing People's Attitudes and Behavior

By carrying out the following steps, operators can change the way they treat and think about the equipment they use:

- Learn to discover abnormalities.
- Make concrete repairs and improvements.
- Make improvements based on clearly defined points.
- Confirm positive results.

Only after people have undergone the hard work of devising, implementing, and maintaining improvements, and only when they have enjoyed the thrill of success, can they begin to treat their equipment in a new and better way. Gradually, they come to understand its original, ideal conditions and realize how to maintain them. In other words, they come to truly understand the importance of daily cleaning, oiling, and precision checks. Then they are keen to keep up with maintenance activities.

So by working to change the equipment, they have also changed their attitudes and behavior toward the equipment. During this process, the operators learn how to keep it in top shape, and having figured this out by themselves, they take pride in their knowledge and are sure to put it into practice. Conversely, people who do not manage to change their equipment will probably not change their attitudes or their behavior toward it. When equipment is changed, people are changed.

Changing the Workplace

Once operators have developed a sharp eye for abnormalities, there is no need to stop with their equipment. They can then focus on everything around it — jigs, tools, processing conditions, control systems, and so on. These peripheral aspects of the workplace are also awash with abnormalities, and having seen them, the operators know that prompt action must be taken to prevent them from developing into big problems. So the first step to changing the workplace is taken when operators begin to notice and list the myriad things that need improvement.

In making improvements, the completion of each step brings you to a new step with new problems. For example, suppose it is discovered that the cycle time needs to be accelerated. This itself creates a new set of problems. To deal with them, it is necessary to figure out what can be done by the workers, what must be handled by the technical staff, and how the solution should be carried out. Soon you get used to each step bringing new problems, and this becomes a natural part of improving the overall quality of the workplace.

In summary, changing the equipment leads to changing attitudes and behaviors, which in turn leads to improving the overall quality of the workplace. These three changes — in the equipment, the people, and the workplace — are what TPM is all about.

4

Approach to Equipment Efficiency Improvement

THE SIX BIG LOSSES: STUMBLING BLOCKS ON THE ROAD TO HIGHER EQUIPMENT EFFICIENCY

One of the goals of TPM is to improve equipment efficiency, and this chapter describes the TPM approach to achieving that goal.

Basically, there are two ways to improve equipment efficiency: a positive way and a negative way. The positive way is by making the most of the functions and performance features of the equipment. The negative way is by eliminating the obstacles to efficiency — obstacles that, in TPM, are called the six big losses. They are

1. Breakdown losses
2. Setup and adjustment losses
3. Idling and minor stoppage losses
4. Reduced speed losses
5. Quality defects and rework
6. Startup/yield losses (reduced yield between machine startup and stable production)

In a machine factory the best way to assess startup/yield losses is through blade and tool loss, because yield loss is primarily due to the service life of blades, drill bits, and other tools. If these items are not replaced when damaged, or if changeover timing is incorrect, there is a corresponding increase in quality defects and rework. This chapter examines the six big losses one by one, and discusses how to minimize or eliminate them completely.

BREAKDOWN LOSSES

Breakdowns are by far the biggest of the six big losses. There are two kinds: failed-function and reduced-function.

Failed-function breakdowns tend to occur sporadically (suddenly), and they are easy to notice because they are relatively dramatic. On the other hand, reduced-function breakdowns enable the equipment to continue operating, but at a reduced level of efficiency. A simple example is a fluorescent lamp that begins to dim or flicker. Very often, reduced-function breakdowns can be discovered only by keen observation. But when they are overlooked, they give rise to idling and minor stoppages, rework, reduced speed, and other problems, and they can become the cause of sporadic, failed-function breakdowns.

In general, breakdowns are caused by all sorts of factors, but we usually notice only the big defects and overlook the myriad slight defects that also contribute to them. Obviously, the big defects deserve attention, but the slight defects deserve equal attention because they accumulate, causing breakdowns also. In fact, many come about simply because seemingly minor things such as loose screws, abrasion, debris, and contaminants are ignored and their effects accumulate until they affect the efficiency of the equipment. The problem of slight defects is discussed in greater detail in Chapter 6.

The Zero Breakdowns Target

To reach the target of zero breakdowns, carry out the following seven actions.

1. Prevent Accelerated Deterioration

Accelerated deterioration is simply deterioration artificially boosted, such as in workshops where equipment overheats because it is not oiled as often as it should be or where equipment is not checked and tightened. Soon looseness in one part affects others, producing a chain reaction eventually leading to a breakdown. When accelerated deterioration is left unchecked, equipment life gets shorter and breakdowns occur; in fact, the majority are caused by accelerated deterioration. Most workshops are rife with it, and it should not be surprising that breakdowns occur as often as they do. So, the first decisive step toward reducing breakdowns is obviously to eliminate accelerated deterioration.

2. Maintain Basic Equipment Conditions

There are three basic activities — cleaning, lubricating, and bolt tightening — that must be performed to maintain basic equipment conditions. If these are not maintained, the workshop will certainly experience lots of breakdowns.

There are various reasons why workers fail to maintain basic equipment conditions. Sometimes they do not know how. Sometimes they do know how, but are too unconcerned or preoccupied to be bothered. Those who do not know need to be taught — but they need to be taught not only how to do the basic maintenance activities, but also why they are so important. Sometimes workers really want to maintain basic equipment conditions but for some reason find it too difficult. For example, checking a machine may require time-consuming disassembly procedures such as removing a bolted-down cover or getting up on a high ladder, platform, or other dangerous procedure. In such cases, there is no choice but to improve the equipment so it can be maintained more easily.

3. Maintain Operating Conditions

Many breakdowns are caused by equipment that must "strain" to operate beyond its normal range because correct conditions are not maintained. Operating equipment under conditions exceeding the limits specified in the operating manual — such as overloading it by allowing hydraulic fluid to overheat — or using 24V power when 12V power is specified is practically asking for breakdowns. This is why maintaining correct operating conditions is so important.

4. Improve Maintenance Quality

Sometimes breakdowns occur in recently replaced or repaired parts because the maintenance worker did not possess the skills necessary to perform the repair or installation correctly. To prevent these mistakes, raise skill levels through training, thereby improving the quality of maintenance work.

5. Take Repair Work beyond Quick-Fix Measures

Repair work is usually focused solely on getting the equipment up and running quickly, without much concern for the root causes of the breakdown. For example, if the most obvious cause was a broken bolt that held a cylinder in place, the repair work often consists of simply replacing the bolt without looking into *why* it broke. Obviously, such an approach only invites a recurrence of the same problem. What's missing here is an attitude that seeks the root cause — which, admittedly, cannot always be found. Without this, however, there cannot be the thorough maintenance required by TPM.

6. Correct Design Weaknesses

One reason breakdowns become chronic is that there is not enough investigation into the weaknesses built into the equipment design, such as poorly designed mechanisms, bad system configurations, or the incorrect selection of materials. All too often there is either no investigation at all into the design flaws or it does not dig deeply enough to uncover their full implications. As a result, maintenance is not improvement-oriented, and breakdowns become chronic.

7. Learn as Much as Possible from Each Breakdown

Once a breakdown has occurred, be certain to learn everything you can. By studying the causes, pre-existing conditions, and correctness of prior methods of checking and making repairs, much can be learned about how to prevent the breakdown from happening again, not only in the equipment at hand, but in similar models.

There are many things to be learned from a breakdown, and it is sad indeed that these lessons are so seldom put to good use. Quite often breakdown reports are only filed away and forgotten instead of used for future reference. Learn to get the most out of such reference material, because it can show maintenance workers and operators what they can do to prevent breakdowns.

All seven points just described must be part of any attempt to reach the goal of zero breakdowns.

SETUP AND ADJUSTMENT LOSSES

Setup and adjustment losses are stoppage losses occurring during setup procedures such as retooling, etc. Setup and

adjustment time is the time required for stopping current production and setting up for production of the next product.
Adjustments tend to use the greatest amount of this time, and in
any company these are of two types — difficult and unavoidable. In other words, people are loath to study adjustments and
therefore seldom study them fully.

The Zero Adjustments Goal

Sometimes adjustments are required because of a lack of
rigidity or some mechanical deficiency. However, in trying to
reduce their number, first look into the adjustment mechanisms,
and divide adjustments into the avoidable (improvable) and the
unavoidable (not improvable). On the average, at a typical factory
70 to 80 percent of adjustments are avoidable and might include
the following:

- Adjustments needed because of an accumulation of
  slight errors in precision, for example, repeated imprecise
  jig or equipment settings.
- Adjustments needed when standards are inconsistent or
  when measurement and quantification methods have not
  been standardized.

Equipment able to turn out nondefective products right
from the start would indicate that zero adjustments had been
achieved. To reach this goal studies must be made and steps
must be taken from a variety of perspectives. What follows
describes two such steps on the road to zero adjustments.

1. Review Precision Settings for Equipment, Jigs, and Tools

In many cases adjustments can be scaled down consider-
ably simply by improving the precision settings of the equipment, jigs, and tools. This is because the accumulation of
imprecise settings creates the need for many otherwise avoidable adjustments.

Typically, shims and liners are used to adjust the precision of various mechanisms; however, this is not a very easy way to make adjustments. Also, when the equipment starts to rattle, operators will often try to compensate, using it as best they can. Whether the imprecision exists only in certain parts or is more widespread, you cannot eliminate it until you find out exactly where it is and how it can be corrected. Also, since the range of precision varies with each piece of equipment, you must carry out separate precision studies for each.

2. Promote Standardization

Lack of consistency in the standards for measurement, quantification, and other operation and maintenance procedures is another cause of avoidable adjustments. The solution is to set clear, consistent, and precise standards for all procedures. In addition, promote standard tool usage as well as assembly and installation methods.

IDLING AND MINOR STOPPAGE LOSSES

Unlike ordinary breakdowns, idling and minor stoppages are caused by temporary problems in the equipment. For example, a workpiece may jam in a chute, or a quality control sensor may temporarily shut down the equipment. As soon as someone removes the jammed workpiece or resets the sensor, it operates normally again. Therefore idling and minor stoppages are qualitatively different from ordinary breakdowns, but they often interfere with efficiency, especially in an automated processing, assembly, or conveyor machine.

Because idling and minor stoppages can usually be restored quite simply, they tend to be overlooked and not regarded as loss. But they are, indeed, losses and this must be made obvious to everyone concerned. However, even after this is pointed out, idling and minor stoppage losses may still be difficult to understand *quantitatively*, and until it is clearly understood just how much of a hindrance they are, thorough measures to eliminate them cannot be devised.

In factories with many equipment units, each instance of idling or minor stoppage will require time to correct, but obviously the longer it takes, the greater the problem. Today there are more and more completely unmanned factories in which idling and minor stoppages pose a very big problem because no one is there to respond right away. So here the zero idling and minor stoppage goal is essential.

The Zero Idling and Minor Stoppage Goal

Remember the following three points when attempting to eliminate idling and minor stoppages:

1. Carefully Observe What Is Happening

Many attempts to eliminate idling and minor stoppages are stymied by knowing only the *results* of these events and not the phenomena *at the time* of the event. Very seldom is a supervisor watching when a machine idles or has a minor stoppage, since these occur infrequently and unpredictably. Therefore you usually have to infer the conditions that were present on the basis of the results and then create a corrective measure based on those inferences. If it were possible, it would be much better to watch the equipment until it had another problem and only then plan a corrective measure.

2. Correct Slight Defects

Often slight defects are not even recognized as true defects and, even when noticed, are ignored. For example, a chute may clog because it is not properly swept out, has a small dent in the side, or some other minor defect.

When dealing with idling and minor stoppages, it is especially important to look for these minor defects. Eliminating them can cut the number of idling and minor stoppages in half and affect other phenomena relative to their occurrence.

3. Understand the Optimal Conditions

Consider the optimal conditions for a vacuum chuck operation such as routinely done for automatic assembly equipment. Typical problem areas include vacuum pressure, chuck time, and timing. These problems arise because people have simply accepted the current settings without checking to see if they are optimal. Maintaining less than ideal conditions is another good way to invite idling and minor stoppages. So take the time to review the settings and see if better ones can be established.

REDUCED SPEED LOSS

Reduced speed loss occurs when there is a difference between the speed at which a machine is designed to operate and its actual speed. For example, reduced speed loss occurs when operators intentionally slow a machine down because its designed speed results in quality defects or mechanical problems. Generally, factory workers and supervisors are not concerned about reduced speed loss for several reasons:

- The specified (designed) speed is only vaguely defined.
- Different speeds have not been set for different products.
- The specified speed is attainable but not reached.
- The problems arising at the specified speed have not been fully investigated.

Since reduced speed loss *does* have a powerful impact on equipment efficiency, it should be fully investigated. Increasing the equipment speed is a good way to expose problems and therefore can help improve the technical skills needed to overcome these problems. Whether you are trying to eliminate breakdowns or defects, corrective actions against reduced speed loss are similar.

QUALITY DEFECTS AND REWORK

This type of loss is incurred through quality defects and related rework or repair. The usual notion of defective goods is that they are beyond repair — but defects *can* be repaired, although this does incur a loss in terms of work hours.

Among quality defects, those that occur sporadically are more easily understood and therefore easier to act against. As a result, they are seldom left untreated. By contrast, chronic defects are more difficult to understand, often resist corrective measures, and are therefore often overlooked or ignored.

Loss incurred by rework and repair has a huge impact on equipment efficiency. Therefore action against it is one of the most important activities in an effort to eliminate the six big losses.

The Zero Defects Target

Since there are different types of defects — sporadic and chronic — reaching the zero defects target is all the more difficult. Reaching it requires coming up with measures based on a comprehensive understanding of all defects. These will be discussed in more detail in Chapter 6, but for now, note the following four key points for eliminating quality defects:

1. Do not jump to conclusions about causes, and be sure corrective measures treat all causes being considered.
2. Carefully observe current conditions.
3. Review the list of causal factors.
4. Review the search for slight defects, which are usually hidden among other causal factors.

STARTUP/YIELD LOSSES

Startup/yield losses are those incurred because of the reduced yield between the time the machine is started up and when stable production is finally achieved. Often, startup/yield losses are difficult to identify, and their extent varies with the stability of processing conditions, the readiness of jigs and dies, worker training, loss incurred by test operations, and other factors. In any case, this usually adds up to a *lot* of loss.

As with quality defects, a discussion of specific measures against startup/yield losses used in TPM will come later, in Chapter 6.

To summarize, the six big losses described in this chapter constitute a major hindrance to equipment efficiency; therefore, eliminating them will give a correspondingly big boost to efficiency.

5

Loss Calculation Methods and Improvement Targets

It is not hard to find factory managers who can immediately give you their equipment availability figures (operating rate), saying "We're operating at 80 percent," or the like. But the fact is, different companies base their figures on different calculations. This chapter explains how equipment loss is calculated in TPM.

OPERATING TIME

Operating time (the time equipment is actually operating as opposed to loading time and other downtime) is what most people refer to when speaking about equipment availability. This is expressed in the following equation:

$$\text{Availability (operating rate)} = \frac{\text{loading time} - \text{downtime}}{\text{loading time}}$$

In this case, loading time is the daily (or monthly) operating time minus all forms of non-operating time — breaks in the production schedule, stoppages for routine maintenance, morning

49

meetings, and other routine stoppages. Downtime is the total time taken for stoppages such as breakdowns, retooling, adjustments, blade and drill bit replacement, and so on.

For instance, suppose the loading time for a given day is 460 minutes, and downtime totals 100 minutes (60 minutes due to breakdowns, 20 minutes for retooling, and 20 minutes due to adjustments). Operating time for the day would therefore be 460 minus 100, or 360 minutes.

The availability (operating rate) can then be calculated as:

$$\text{Availability} = \frac{360}{460} \times 100 = 78\%$$

However, 78 percent availability (operating rate) does not correctly indicate actual operating conditions. While it does account for breakdown loss, it does not account for defects, speed loss, and other loss factors. The following describes how TPM deals with this problem.

PERFORMANCE RATE

Performance rate is based on the operating speed rate and the net operating time. Operating speed rate is the ratio of the *ideal* speed of the equipment (in terms of cycle time or strokes) to its *actual* speed. In other words, it shows the speed at which the equipment is actually operating relative to its ideal speed (its designed speed, or ideal cycle time). When the performance rate shows a speed reduction, it reflects some kind of loss. We can use the following equation to define operating speed rate:

$$\text{Operating rate speed} = \frac{\text{ideal cycle time}}{\text{actual cycle}}$$

Net operating time is the time during which equipment is being operated at a constant speed within a specified period. Here the issue is not how fast the equipment is operating relative to the ideal speed, but how stable and constant the speed remains over a long period of time. Net operating time can therefore be used to calculate loss due to idling and minor stoppages, or other problems not usually mentioned in the daily log.

The formula for net operating time is as follows:

$$\text{Net operating time} = \frac{\text{output} \times \text{actual cycle time}}{\text{loading time} - \text{downtime}}$$

We can then calculate the performance rate as follows:

$$\text{Performance rate} = \text{Operating speed rate} \times \text{Net operating time}$$

OVERALL EQUIPMENT EFFECTIVENESS

As you can see, there are many ways to calculate equipment loss. In TPM, the availability, performance, and quality figures are multiplied to arrive at a measurement of the overall operating condition of the equipment. This can be used for all types of equipment. It is called the "overall equipment effectiveness," and is defined by the following formula:

$$\text{Overall equipment effectiveness} =$$
$$\text{Availability} \times \text{Performance rate} \times \text{Quality rate}$$

Factories that are assessed by this method are generally found to have overall equipment effectiveness ratings between 50 and 60 percent. Figure 5-1 contains a flow chart showing how this works.

The following is a sample set of calculations.

Calculation Example

Operating time for the day:	60 minutes × 8 hours = 480 minutes
Loading time for the day:	460 minutes
Downtime for the day:	60 minutes . . . . . . Downtime components: Retooling (20 min.) Breakdowns (20 min.) Adjustments (20 min.) Rework (2%)
Output for the day:	400 product units
Availability:	$\dfrac{400}{460} \times 100 = 87.0\%$
Ideal cycle time:	0.5 minutes per product unit
Actual cycle time:	0.8 minutes per product unit
Operating speed rate:	$\dfrac{0.5}{0.8} \times 100 = 62.5\%$
Net operating time:	$\dfrac{400 \text{ units} \times 0.8}{400 \text{ minutes}} \times 100 = 80.0\%$

(1 − net operating time) indicates loss due to idling and minor stoppages.

Performance rate:	62.5% × 80.0 = 50.0%
Quality (nondefective) rate:	98.0%
Overall effectiveness:	87.0 × 50.0 × 98.0 = 42.6%

In the preceding example, the very poor overall effectiveness rating of 42.6 percent is due to poor operating speed and poor net operating time. So these calculations suggest the company should find ways to speed up the equipment and eliminate idling and minor stoppages.

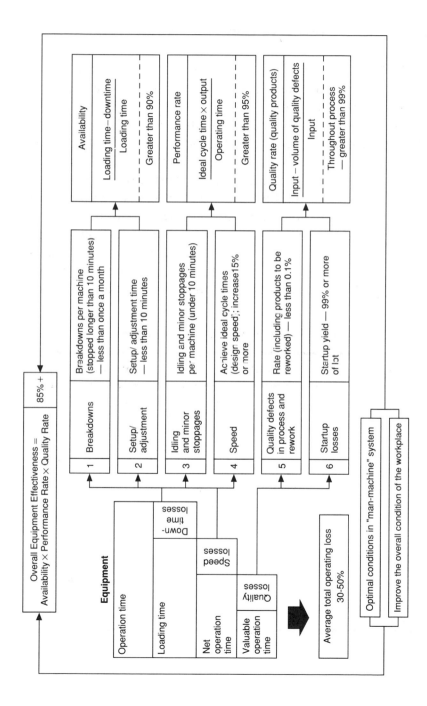

Figure 5-1. Improvement Goals for Chronic Losses

IMPROVEMENT TARGETS FOR THE SIX BIG LOSSES

Table 5-1 lists improvement targets for the six big losses. Figure 5-2 shows the corresponding indicators of improvement in equipment effectiveness.

In TPM, the overall equipment effectiveness is increased by reducing or eliminating losses that affect availability (breakdown, setup, adjustment, and blade or bit replacement), losses that affect performance rate (idling and minor stoppages, reduced speed, and quality defects), and losses that affect the quality rate (quality defects, rework, and startup loss).

Although the six big losses can be found in every workplace, the relative proportion of each will vary depending on equipment characteristics, line configuration, automation conditions, and other factors. For example, if the workplace has an

Table 5-1. Improvement Targets for the Six Big Losses

LOSS	TARGET	DESCRIPTION
1 Breakdown loss	Zero	Breakdown loss must be reduced to zero for all equipment
2 Setup/adjustment loss	Minimize	Minimize setup/adjustment loss by doing single setups lasting less than 10 minutes, and with zero adjustments
3 Speed loss	Zero	Eliminate all differences between the actual and designed conditions of the equipment
4 Idling and minor stoppage loss	Zero	Idling and minor stoppage loss must be completely eliminated in all equipment
5 Quality defects and rework	Zero	Keep such loss within a minimum range in terms of ppm (such as 30 to 100 ppm)
6 Startup loss	Minimize	

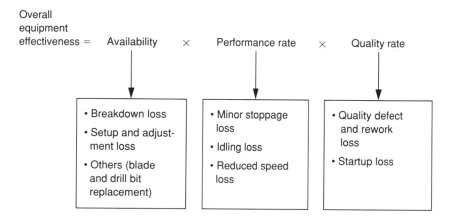

Figure 5-2. Efficiency Index

abundance of setup/adjustment and breakdown loss, it will have an especially poor availability (operating rate). Likewise, a workshop fraught with idling and minor stoppages will have a particularly low performance rate.

Therefore, at any workplace, the approach is to first find out which losses are having the greatest impact on equipment effectiveness, and then address the bulk of the improvement efforts toward those. To do this, follow these steps:

1. Measure the extent of each of the six big losses.
2. Measure how much each loss affects overall equipment effectiveness.
3. Find out what problems stand in the way of improving availability, performance rate, and quality rate.
4. Determine targets and orientations needed to solve problems discovered in Step 3.
5. Find out how higher equipment effectiveness will affect cost-cutting and profit-boosting.

Figure 5-3 illustrates the relation between overall equipment effectiveness and improvement problems in the six big losses.

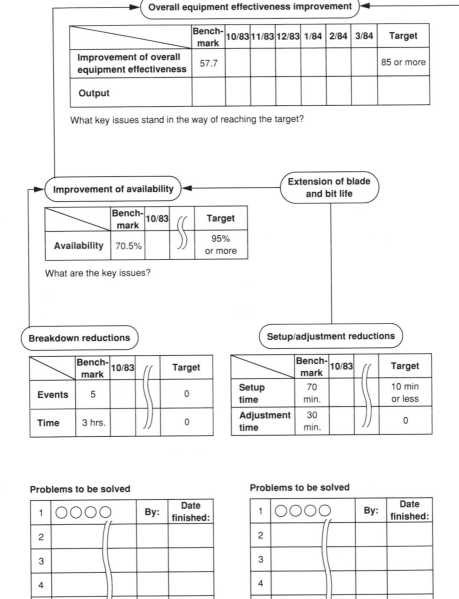

Figure 5-3. Relation between Overall Equipment Effectiveness and the Problems Connected with Six Big Loss Improvement

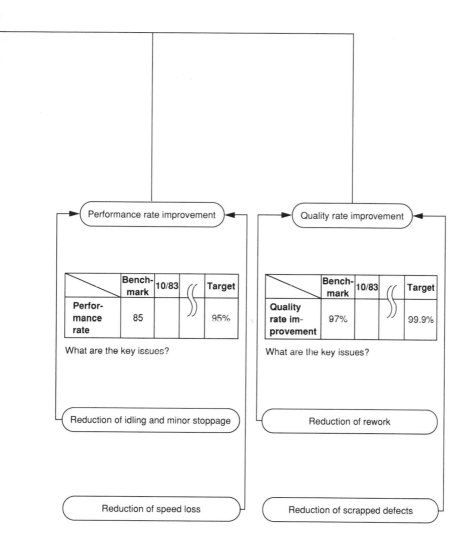

	Bench-mark	10/83		Target
Perfor-mance rate	85			95%

What are the key issues?

Reduction of idling and minor stoppage

Reduction of speed loss

	Bench-mark	10/83		Target
Quality rate im-provement	97%			99.9%

What are the key issues?

Reduction of rework

Reduction of scrapped defects

(The forms showing the benchmarks and problems to be solved are abbreviated since they are the same as the first one shown at left.)

In TPM, "individual improvements" are the activities companies carry out to improve their performance by thoroughly eliminating the six big losses and maximizing overall equipment effectiveness.

6

Approach to Chronic Loss Improvement

Previous chapters have discussed the six big losses — the major obstacles to equipment efficiency. This chapter focuses on chronic loss and the TPM approach to this particularly difficult problem.

UNDERSTANDING CHRONIC LOSS CHARACTERISTICS

Rather than examining chronic loss in all of the six big losses, the focus in this text will be on the two in which chronic loss is most prevalent: breakdowns and quality defects.

Chronic Events and Sporadic Events

As mentioned previously, breakdowns, defects, and other abnormalities occur either sporadically or chronically. Since causes of sporadic abnormalities are relatively easy to find, they are fairly easy to correct. For example, quality defects may suddenly occur when a jig has worn to where it can no longer support the required precision, or when a spindle suddenly vibrates too much, causing unacceptable variations in product dimensions. These sudden changes in conditions can be corrected simply by restoring the condition or component to its original state.

On the other hand, by definition, chronic abnormalities are likely to persist even after corrective measures have been taken. This is because they rarely have just one cause, which makes establishing clear-cut cause-and-effect relationships much more difficult. And this makes it equally difficult to devise effective improvements (see Figure 6-1).

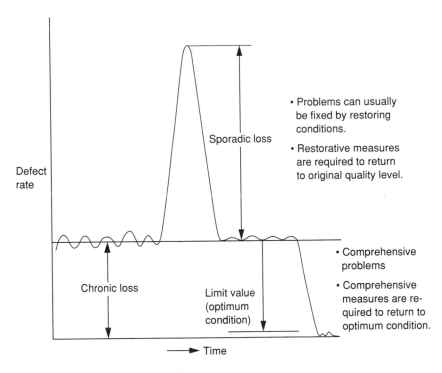

Figure 6-1. Difference between Sporadic Loss and Chronic Loss

Characteristics of Chronic Loss

In any attempt to correct a chronic loss, understanding its characteristics is most important (see Figure 6-2). These can be summed up as follows:

- A chronic problem with just one identifiable cause still has many other factors that can (and do) become causes, and these can change from one occurrence to the next.
- When a chronic problem has multiple causes, the combination can change from one occurrence of the problem to the next.

When a chronic problem has just one identifiable cause, it could be one among many, *all* of which — individually — could produce the same problem. So, any two occurrences could have very different causes. Suppose you prepared a list of ten possible causes for a particular abnormality and identified them as causes A through J. Each time it occurs, the cause may be one of ten. This means if you attack the problem targeting only one cause, you cannot expect very good results.

Consider the following example. The precision of the honed surface finish on inner and outer ball grooves in ball bearing housings is a major factor in determining quality. In a hypothetical case, the surface honing process has a 1 to 2 percent defect rate from rough spots left on the surface. The possible causes include the shape of the honing grinder, the method used for attaching it, dress defects, a loose grinder holder, a loose work spindle, imprecise curve grinding, various processing conditions, and so on. In short, possible causes range from things done in the previous process (such as curve grinding) to things done during a setup procedure, such as attaching the grinder. But the *actual* cause of the abnormality can change from one instance to the next. Consequently, the only way to really

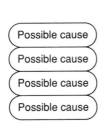

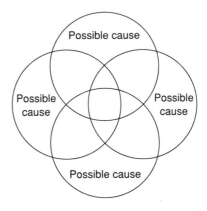

Only one cause,
but many possible causes

Combination of causes,
but many possible combinations

Figure 6-2. Characteristics of Chronic Loss

end a chronic loss problem is to take corrective action against *all* possible causes by restoring them to their original conditions, and preventing any deviation from those conditions.

Solving problems is not too difficult if all their causes are easily identified, but when some are not, it is necessary to resort to a more comprehensive approach.

When a chronic problem has multiple causes several can overlap, combining to create the problem. To make matters worse, the combination can change from one instance to the next; for example, the problem may have been due to causes A, B, and C the last time, but now it is due to A, C, G, and H.

Consider a process that uses an internal cylindrical grinding machine to grind and polish certain components. It is suffering from chronic defects related to uneven roundness of the processed components. The possible overlapping causes include dimensional variations in the material itself, wearing down of the reference board used for attaching the workpiece, vibration of the grinding spindle, and insufficient quill hardness. Since all

these may be contributing to any single occurrence of the defect, corrective actions must be taken against *all* of them, without giving in to the temptation to narrow them down to just one or even a few.

At all too many factories, people respond to chronic problems before they have gained an adequate understanding of the loss, so their improvement efforts do not produce the desired results. The major pitfall is that people narrow their focus too much, deciding what caused the problem before they have fully understood it. Once they believe they have identified the cause or causes, they direct corrective measures only toward those. Naturally they miss all they failed to identify. So even when they succeed in correcting the causes they target, others remain unidentified or ignored, meaning that the effect can only be temporary, and the chronic loss will recur. Only by developing a thorough understanding of the chronic loss characteristics can this be avoided.

Reduction of Chronic Loss

As demonstrated in the preceding examples, three things should be considered when acting to reduce chronic loss.

1. Acquire a thorough understanding of the phenomena. Very few factories are staffed by people conscientious enough to thoroughly examine and categorize defect phenomena. Most factories fail to fully understand them, which usually means a failure to notice key factors like defect patterns, different components involved, and times at which the phenomena occur. Often people devise corrective measures before they have even thought about the phenomena or the mechanisms behind their occurrence. Little wonder these hastily devised measures do little to reduce chronic loss.

2. Thoroughly review the list of causes. If the phenomena are not thoroughly examined, some causes are likely to be overlooked. Corrective measures, therefore, will not be taken to deal with them, and things may end up being dealt with that have nothing to do with the actual problem. Avoiding this requires a thorough, analytical approach, listing all causes that could possibly relate to the problem at hand.

3. Uncover any slight defects hidden within the possible causes. Sometimes a close examination of one cause reveals evidence of other, previously unnoticed defects. People still tend to overlook these "slight" defects because they have not developed a critical eye — and an awareness of the importance of correcting them.

Figure 6-3 summarizes this discussion of chronic loss improvements.

The following sections provide a closer look at the key elements in the summary shown in Figure 6-3, namely P-M analysis, finding out what the optimal conditions are, and restoring optimal conditions.

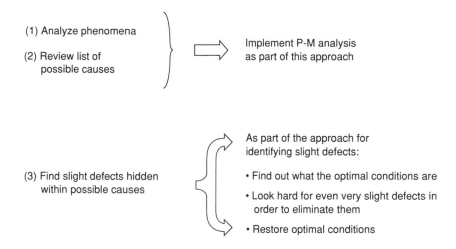

(1) Analyze phenomena

(2) Review list of
     possible causes

Implement P-M analysis
as part of this approach

(3) Find slight defects hidden
     within possible causes

As part of the approach for
identifying slight defects:

• Find out what the optimal conditions are

• Look hard for even very slight defects in
   order to eliminate them

• Restore optimal conditions

Figure 6-3. Approach to Chronic Loss Improvement

HOW TO IMPLEMENT P-M ANALYSIS

This section describes a step-by-step approach to P-M analysis.

Definition*

Cause and effect diagrams are commonly used for improvement, and they often produce good results. However, when the problem is complicated, these begin to show their limitations. One tendency is to list possible causes without fully understanding the phenomena. Even when the list of possible causes is based on a consideration of the 4M's (machine, material, man, and method), if a full analysis has not been performed, unrelated

---

* The *P* in *P-M analysis* stands for "phenomena" and "physical," as in "looking at phenomena in physical terms." The *M* stands for mechanism, machine, man, and material, which are interrelated factors to be studied.

causes tend to be listed and important related ones are often overlooked.

P-M analysis was developed to overcome this limitation of cause and effect diagrams and consists of the following steps:

Step 1: Clarify the Phenomena

To understand these phenomena, examine how they occur, study the relevant workshop conditions, consider the affected parts, the differences between equipment models, and so on. Once you have identified all these factors, then categorize them, and organize them into patterns.

Step 2: Do a Physical Analysis of the Phenomena

When doing a physical analysis, look at the phenomena from various angles and come to understand them in terms of physical principles. For example, if an object is being damaged, this can be explained by the principle that when two objects contact each other, the one not strong enough to withstand the shock will be damaged. Accordingly, study all places of contact or shock thoroughly to identify the cause of the damage and to determine where improvements are needed.

The point here is that the first step toward understanding phenomena is looking at their physical principles. There are three good reasons for this. First of all, the way you examine the phenomena affects the way you deal with their causes. Second, taking a logical, systematic approach can avoid careless over-sights. And finally, this helps avoid making intuitive judgments.

Step 3: Define the Conditions that Produce the Phenomena

Once you have described phenomena according to physical principles, ask questions about the conditions necessary to produce them. Once these are defined, consider all situations in which they prevail.

Often people fail to consider all the existing conditions, and this is reflected in their corrective actions, which fail to reduce the breakdown, defect, or other problem at hand.

Step 4: List the Factors that Cause Each Condition

In this step, identify and list the factors related to each condition in Step 3 such as equipment, material, work methods, and the people involved. Here it is important to think systematically about all factors that may give rise to each condition.

At this point how much each factor affects each condition is unimportant. For now, simply list all factors. In doing this, carefully study such matters as equipment mechanisms, operating principles, machine part functions, and the precision required to maintain those functions. People often overlook important factors just because they are not aware of these matters.

Step 5: Plan the Investigation

Carefully plan the study method, measurement method, and scope of study for each factor identified in earlier steps.

Step 6: Identify Specific Abnormalities

Using the study method planned in Step 5, identify specific abnormalities for each factor. However, instead of using the traditional approach, take into account the optimal conditions and the possibility of slight defects.

Maintain a critical attitude when looking for abnormalities. For example, think about the optimal conditions for the equipment functions you are concerned with, then ask why they do not exist. Most of all, resist the temptation to stop the search for abnormalities after finding one or two major ones. The key to success lies in completely investigating all factors.

Step 7: Draft Improvement Plans

You are now ready to draft improvement plans for the identified abnormalities — for instance, overhauling or replacing parts. However, often the simple restoration of optimal conditions is not enough; sometimes insufficient hardness in certain parts or poorly designed mechanisms make partial remodeling of the equipment necessary, too.

Example of P-M Analysis

At an end mill factory a cylindrical grinding machine grinds the exterior of quench-hardened round bars. This process has been plagued by cylindricality defects, prompting workers to make frequent adjustments, but they have not prevented defects from recurring (see Figure 6-4 and Table 6-1).

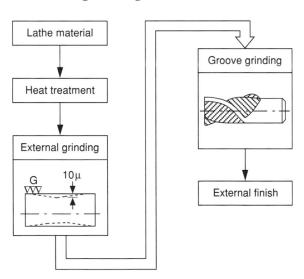

Figure 6-4. Process Outline

The following is a study of this case according to the P-M analysis previously described.

Step 1: Clarify the Phenomena

After a careful look at the phenomena the workers determined there were two types of cylindricality defects, the first concerning tapering of certain parts of the workpiece, and the second concerning overall tapering.

Step 2: Physically Analyze the Phenomena

They reasoned that the imprecision in cylindricality could be due either to an overall lack of axial parallelism between the workpiece and the grinder, or partial variation in axial parallelism.

Put another way, if correct axial parallelism is maintained between the workpiece and the grinder, cylindricality will remain precise. Causes of defective axial parallelism could include vibration of the equipment, imprecise adjustments by the operators, or slippage of the workpiece.

At this point it might be helpful to refer to another P-M analysis table. This concerns slippage of batteries at a battery factory rotating table (see Table 6-2).

Step 3: Define the Conditions that Produce the Phenomena

In Steps 1 and 2 they discovered the cylindricality defects were being caused either by an overall lack of axial parallelism between the workpiece and the grinder or by an occasional variation in parallelism.

They thought about various conditions that could contribute to either parallelism problem and came up with three: (1) the centers were not operating precisely enough, (2) equipment precision was inadequate, (3) the operators were making adjustment errors.

Table 6-1. P-M Analysis of Cylindrical Grinding Machine

Target Phenomenon: Poor cylindricality in workpiece

Physical Description: Variation in axial alignment between workpiece and grinding spindle

Existing Conditions	Factors (possible causes)	Investigation Results	Improvement Measure
1. Problems with centers	(1) Friction on centers	(1) After checking all of the centers, some were found to have worn edges, and the operators had been using these centers without being aware of their worn condition.	(1) Discard or regrind and reuse
	(2) Damaged centers	(2) As in (1) above, the operators were unaware of cracked and otherwise damaged centers.	(2) Discard or regrind and reuse
	(3) Variation in length of centers	(3) Length measurements revealed ten different lengths among the centers.	(3) Consolidate into three lengths: 30mm, 35mm, and 45mm
	(4) Shape of center hole tip	(4) As shown below, it is difficult to see the center hole, which can easily result in damage when the workpiece is attached.	(4) Chamfered centers to make center holes easier to see.

Chamfered section

Existing Conditions	Factors (possible causes)	Investigation Results	Improvement Measure
	(5) Vibration against tapered surfaces of centers	(5) After checking all of the centers, vibration was found in the range of 35 to 90 microns	(5) Discard centers with large vibration values, and change the manufacturing sequence to "supply raw material → lathe → chamfer → heat treatment → setup → grinding" to maintain vibration within 10 microns.
	(6) Center loading method	(6) No standard method has been set for loading centers, therefore the centers were sometimes loaded as shown below.	(6) The center loading method shown below was established as the standard method.

Grinder   Grinder

| | (7) Collision between center and grinder | (7) Discovered collisions between center and grinder | (7) Changed operating manual to require use of a square to check center loading precision. |

Grinder

Table 6-1. P-M Analysis of Cylindrical Grinding Machine (cont.)

Existing Conditions	Factors (possible causes)	Investigation Results	Improvement Measure
2. Lack of equipment precision	(1) Variation in height of centers	(1) Measured 110-micron positive differential in relative height of centers +110μ 0 100mm	(1) Reduced to 20-micron negative differential 0 20μ 100mm
	(2) Parallelism between centers	(2) Measured 800-micron differential in parallelism between centers +80μ −720μ 100mm	(2) Reduced to 40-micron differential +40μ +80μ 100mm
	(3) Loose handle control	(3) Loose handle creates 30-micron imprecision in control	(3) Reduced handle control imprecision to 5 microns
	(4) Weak spring in spring coupler	(4) Observed tendency for workpiece to slip away under grinding pressure	(4) Replaced spring with one that is three times stronger, and this greatly reduced slippage.
	(5) Loose section of lathe table	(5) 40-micron vibration in table produces differential in clockwise rotation, which prevents dial gauge from reading taper adjustment. Table Dial gauge 40μ Bed	(5) Installed spring to hold table and maintain 40-micron vibration in the direction of the gauge. 40μ Spring Dial gauge is able to read taper adjustment when lathe turns either clockwise or counterclockwise.
	(6) Problem in spring coupler stabilizing method	(6) Nonstandard stabilizing jig was being used, which caused a gap to exist between the spring coupler and the stabilizing jig.	(6) Replaced nonstandard jig with standard jig to close gap.

Table 6-2. Example of P-M Analysis

Target Phenomenon: Slippage of batteries on rotating table

Physical Description: External condition such as shock, friction, vibration, etc. causes
centrifugal center to shift and go off balance.

Existing Conditions	Factors (possible causes)
1. Conditions that cause friction	1. Left blank
• Contact between rotating table and workpiece	2-1 Surface conditions of table
• Condition of workpiece (shape of bottom surface, adhesion of foreign matter, etc.)	2-2 Flatness of table
	2-3 Deflection of table
	2-4 Inconsistent rotation of table
2. Conditions that cause vibration	2-5 Shape, position, or angle of peripheral guide
• Caused by rotating table (belt flap, deflection, etc.)	2-6 Surface conditions of guide
• Contact between rotating table and peripheral guide	2-7 Contact condition between table and peripheral guide
3. Conditions that cause shock	3. Left blank

Step 4: List the Factors that Cause Each Condition

At this step they listed all causes that could possibly be related to each condition. Causes related to imprecision in the centers included external factors like friction, damage, and tip shape, dimensional precision factors such as the protrusion length of the center, vibration of the taper surface, and possible errors in the operator's center loading method.

They also listed equipment-precision factors such as height differences between centers, differences in axial parallelism between centers, loose handle control, inadequate spring strength in the spring coupler, and vibration in the table lathe.

Step 5: Plan the Investigation

At this point, they decided what measurement and investigative steps were needed to study these causes. Their purpose was to locate any slight defects that might exist, so they needed accurate, yet simple methods to find them.

They approached the matter of relative height difference between centers by attaching a test arbor and lining up both ends with reference points on the table, then used a height gauge to measure the distance between the periphery and the table surface.

Likewise, they used their five senses and other measurement instruments to investigate each possible cause.

Step 6: Identify Specific Abnormalities

They selected all defects and *apparent* defects they could find, which, in this case, totaled 15.

Step 7: Draft Improvement Plans

It is vital that responses are made to *all* the selected defects. As mentioned earlier, people often make the mistake of looking around the workshop, finding two or three defects, and addressing only those, ignoring all the *hidden* defects.

The improvement team could not hope to achieve zero defects unless they took corrective measures against all 15 they identified. Looking over descriptions of the improvements, it is impossible to tell which had the greatest effect on eliminating the defects. In fact, there is little point in trying to discover which improvement was most effective. All that can be said is that this was a typical example of comprehensive improvement that succeeded in reaching the goal of zero defects by removing each little defect.

APPROACH TO DISCOVERING SLIGHT DEFECTS

This section describes TPM's approach toward discovering slight defects. The two key elements are a search for optimal conditions *and* a search for slight defects.

Search for Optimal Conditions

Optimal conditions means the conditions in which equipment operates at its highest level — conditions most serviceable according to engineering principles and theories and ideal for equipment functioning. For the purposes of this discussion, these can be divided into two categories: necessary and desirable.

Necessary conditions are the minimum required to support equipment operation. Desirable conditions are not *essential*, but they can help avoid breakdowns and defects.

Optimal conditions must naturally include all those deemed necessary but must also include desirable ones. People tend to emphasize necessary conditions and overlook desirable ones, but this is a big mistake from the perspective of TPM.

Here are some examples.

V-Belt Example

For this example a pulley arrangement accommodates three V-belts. The necessary conditions for correct V-belt operation are that at least one belt is installed, and the belt(s) must meet all standards.

Desirable conditions include the following:

- All three V-belts should be installed for operation.
- All three V-belts should have equal tension.
- The belts should be free of cracks and grease marks.
- The pulley should be free of abrasion.

- There should be proper alignment between motor and speed reducers.

Failure to establish and maintain these conditions increases the risk of slippage, inconsistent rotation, shortened service life, and other problems.

Grease Supply Example

The only necessary condition in this example is that grease be applied at specified locations.

Desirable conditions include the following:

- The grease nipple should be kept clean.
- The area around the grease fitting should be wiped clean after each application.
- The condition of the used lubricant (color, etc.) and the volume level should be checked.
- Used lubricant should be disposed of properly.

- An estimate should be made of how many days the lubricant takes to reach the end of the piping.
- The grease container should be kept clean and free of dirt.

Limit Switch Example

There is only one necessary condition — that the limit switch be installed and operated as specified.

Desirable conditions include the following:

- The dogs and levers should be aligned in a straight line.
- The areas around dogs and levers should not be too strong (they should allow a lever movement angle of about 30 degrees).
- The brackets should be tightly fastened.

As seen from these examples, to restore and keep equipment in its original, optimal state, maintaining necessary and desirable conditions is essential.

Using Optimal Conditions as an Indicator of Slight Defects

This section describes a way of using optimal conditions to reveal slight defects in equipment. First describe the optimal conditions (desirable conditions) for each function of the jig, then compare these to the actual conditions. A discrepancy between optimal and actual conditions indicates slight defects exist.

Using jigs as an example, determine the optimal conditions by studying ideal conditions for surface coarseness, dimensional precision, attachment method, movement conditions, and clamping strength. Then compare these with actual conditions of the jig to see where slight defects have created the discrepancy.

Many factories do not even employ the standard of optimal conditions, or if they do, there are errors in the way they determine, standardize, or maintain them. When equipment is operated without an adequate understanding of its ideal conditions, then breakdowns, defects, and rework are much more likely to occur.

Points for Studying Optimal Conditions

See Figure 6-5 with reference to the following points related to the study of optimal conditions.

Dimensional Precision. Is the dimensional precision of individual equipment components correct?

External Shape and Appearance. Do components have the correct external appearance and shape? For example, are they free of dirt and rust? Are they properly aligned?

Assembly Precision. Is the assembly precision totally correct? Often individual components may have adequate precision, but as assembled products they lose it. Problem areas can include imprecise positioning of reference surfaces or attachment points, etc.

Material Quality and Strength. Is the material suitable, or would some other material extend equipment life? Is the material hard enough?

Equipment Functions. Is each equipment component functioning normally and within correct use range limits (upper and lower)?

Workshop Environment. Is the equipment installed in a good area? Is the area excessively hot, cold, or dirty? Does it meet specifications for maintenance?

Use Conditions. Is the equipment being used in optimal processing conditions?

Installation Precision. Does the installation precision meet specifications such as those requiring flat, even surfaces and low vibration levels?

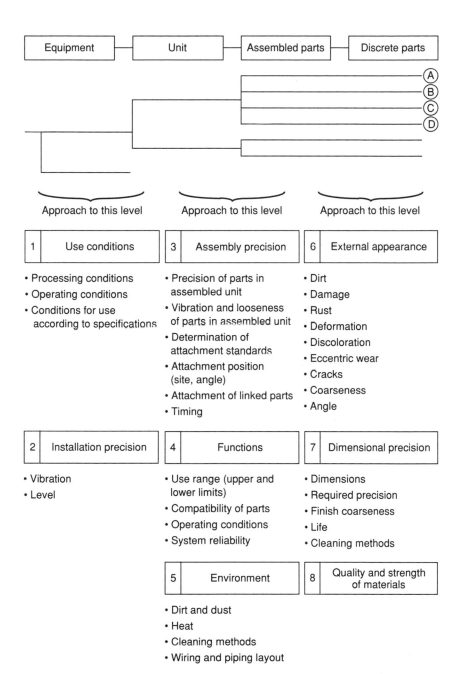

Figure 6-5. Investigation of Optimal Conditions

Clearly Differentiate between Normal and Abnormal

Drawing a clear line between normal and abnormal is a very important part of any investigation into optimal conditions. When the contrast is great, telling them apart is not hard. But when the contrast is slight, normal and abnormal become harder to determine. Consider a situation where an incorrectly attached part vibrates the equipment. If the vibration is bad enough, anyone would tell there is something abnormal. However, if it is only slight, some might consider it abnormal, while others might not.

There is always a very large chance that equipment problems will occur simply because of the different ways in which people understand normal and abnormal. As a result, a clear-cut distinction must be made between them (see Figure 6-6).

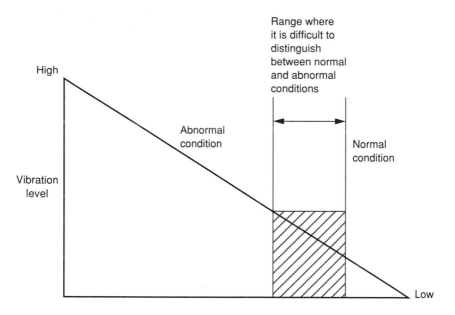

Figure 6-6. Normal and Abnormal Conditions

Slight Defects

The next important step is approaching chronic loss improvement by eliminating slight defects. There is a tendency to notice only major defects in equipment, and to end improvement efforts when these are eliminated. But the job is not finished until you have dealt with slight defects that can cause chronic product defects or equipment breakdowns without even being recognized as defects. That is why it is so important to recognize not only the large defects but also the small ones.

Definition of Slight Defects

Slight defects are equipment abnormalities small enough to be debatable as defects, since each has only a tiny influence on major problems. Traditionally, slight defects were ignored as insignificant, because each one had such little effect on product quality defects, equipment breakdowns, idling, and minor stoppages. Examples are things like dirt, grime, vibration, and slightly excessive abrasion (such as 4 percent instead of the specified 3 percent). You may be unable to tell how much influence each defect has, but at least recognize, theoretically, that they have *some* influence.

For example, suppose an NC lathe occasionally operates a bit strangely. This can be caused by such minor things as a loose screw, rust buildup at a critical location, or a contact that has become defective due to an accumulation of dirt or dust. In such cases just a little dirt, rust, or looseness can have a great impact on equipment operation, and that's why slight defects demand the same treatment as more significant ones.

That's an example of just a single defect. There are also cases where several slight defects have a serious cumulative effect. Suppose a certain jig has been damaged, and the operator, not noticing this, keeps using it in his assembly work, resulting in substandard assembly precision. This, in turn, leads to

early wear eventually causing both static and dynamic imprecision in the equipment. Another example is when individual
operators set the origin point on the measurement tools differ-
ently. Or sometimes a minor variation at one phase of production will combine with other slight defects and result in a 1 to 2
percent product defect rate at the end.

In short, the greater the number of slight defects, the harder
it is to identify the sources of whatever problems they collec-
tively cause. Therefore the only resort is to look at every possible
location of slight defects, from jigs to assembly methods and
precision results, thereby minimizing the risk of overlooking
even one.

Successful elimination of slight defects is a prerequisite
for reaching the goals of zero defects and zero breakdowns. To
avoid underestimating their importance, think of them as
major defects.

Importance of Slight Defects

One good reason slight defects are important is that they can accumulate, compounding their results and producing powerful cumulative effects. This can result in a defect greater than all the contributing ones. Even when a defect is very small, it can trigger others, or combine with others to produce a larger effect, or even a chain reaction.

Slight defects, if ignored, can lead to major equipment defects and breakdowns, as well as product defects. They can also result in a higher incidence of accelerated deterioration and rework.

Clues for Finding Slight Defects

There are a few clues for finding slight defects. First of all, study the equipment's physical principles, and use these to help navigate the complicated maze of causes and effects. This means using physical principles to judge desirable conditions, the status of equipment and component functions, and the maintenance of those functions. For example, the function of a chute is to guide workpieces as they are drop-conveyed by their own weight. If the surface of the chute is dirty or damaged, the desirable conditions for the chute are not being maintained, and this is a slight defect. If the dirt or damage begins to affect the condition of the workpieces, the risk of serious problems becomes much greater.

Failure frequently results from approaching chronic problems trying to find their exact causes and the importance of *each* one. Do not be concerned with the impact of each slight defect. It is counterproductive to try to determine their influence on any given problem. Besides being likely to end in failure, this leads people into thinking that slight defects are not very important since their effects cannot be measured. Instead, assume that *all* slight defects have some *small* effect, and therefore must be eliminated.

RESTORATION

The discussion of restoration begins with a description of a related subject, deterioration.

Natural Deterioration and Accelerated Deterioration

There are two types of deterioration: natural and accelerated.

Natural deterioration is the physical wear that occurs in spite of correct use and maintenance. For example, even when the equipment is oiled as required, it will still deteriorate over time.

Accelerated deterioration, on the other hand, is natural deterioration that has been sped up by human causes, such as negligent oiling, checking, or repair. Consequently, accelerated deterioration results in much shorter life expectancy for the equipment.

Unfortunately, accelerated deterioration is a common problem in factories today. A single loose bolt can cause vibration, and as it increases, other parts of the equipment begin to vibrate. Or a limit switch may be covered with cutting fluid and making overly strong contact with the dog, resulting in accelerated deterioration.

Cleaning Is Checking

Cleaning is a very good way to discover deterioration. When cleaning equipment, each part is touched, and this close contact gives an opportunity to discover problems. That is why TPM uses the expression "cleaning is checking" (see Figure 6-7).

Contact with each part of the equipment leads to the discovery of problems such as overheating, vibration, looseness, abnormal noises, dirt, and the like. Wiping away dirt from contact surfaces and removing cutting debris and grease helps put the

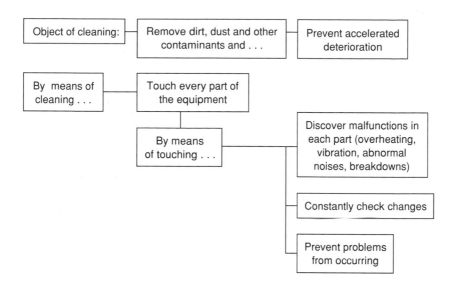

Figure 6-7. Cleaning Is Inspection

brakes on accelerated deterioration. Cleaning is not only an effective way to discover abnormalities but an indispensable means of extending the life expectancy of parts and maintaining precision.

Consider a very common example — washing your car. What's the difference between washing it in an automated car wash and by hand? Not much, as far as superficial considerations go; both will result in a clean exterior. However, a person who washes the car by hand is "checking" it at the same time and is therefore in a much better position to discover tires that are cracked, punctured, or in need of rotation or body areas that are dented or rusty.

The same is true for equipment operators. By washing their equipment manually they can keep close tabs on its condition and discover abnormalities more easily.

Restoration for Prevention of Defects

All equipment parts gradually deteriorate over time. The progress varies according to their characteristics, so some may deteriorate rapidly once they wear beyond a certain "drop-off" point, while others may keep deteriorating gradually (see Figure 6-8). It is important to discover where such drop-off points exist and to be certain to restore equipment that has reached that point.

For example, consider an automatic lathe. The maintenance of a lathe includes static precision characteristics like main spindle deflection, linearity, levelness, and chuck wear. It also includes maintenance of dynamic precision characteristics, such as the routine measurement of vibration values at the main spindle and cutting table. If necessary, it also includes repair of the equipment to restore these values to tolerance ranges. Although

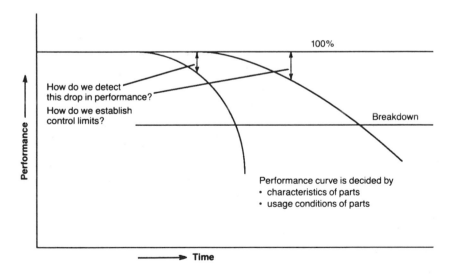

Figure 6-8. Development of Deterioration

measures like these are intended to prevent defects and break-downs, due to the following reasons they are sometimes not thorough:

- There is no method for measuring how far deterioration has progressed.
- There are no criteria for determining how far deterioration *should* be allowed to progress before the equipment is restored.
- Full-fledged restoration methods have not been developed.
- The fully restored conditions of the equipment have not been determined.

Restoration Comes before Improvement

When equipment has a series of breakdowns, people often respond by replacing mechanisms, parts, and/or materials. However, in many cases these measures do no good. You should suspect that the mechanisms, parts, or materials themselves aren't causing the breakdowns, but rather certain conditions have been causing those parts to wear down as well as causing the decline in finishing or assembly precision. Restoring *those* conditions to their proper state will stop the breakdowns, and that is why restoration should always come before replacing mechanisms or parts. Only when restoration measures fail should you consider these kinds of improvements.

This concludes the discussion of the TPM approach to chronic loss improvement. Here is a brief review of the points just discussed.

Most important in making chronic loss improvements is to carefully identify relevant phenomena and analyze them in terms of physical principles. How you analyze phenomena will affect the way you identify their causes. At this stage, to avoid overlooking those that require attention, proceed very carefully.

P-M analysis is a very good tool for ensuring a thorough and effective analysis.

Many factories are plagued by product defects and equipment breakdowns because they overlook defects in their equipment and jigs. They have not developed a sharp eye for spotting equipment defects and do not even know *how* to look for them.

Restoration is very important to prevent equipment defects. You cannot hope to achieve the zero defect/zero breakdown goal without eliminating accelerated deterioration, maintaining and measuring natural deterioration, and restoring the equipment whenever natural deterioration progresses to a certain point. This is a must if defects and breakdowns are to be prevented.

Chronic loss is a major obstacle to equipment efficiency, so by making chronic loss improvements, overall efficiency can be increased, naturally leading to higher profitability.

Having mastered the TPM approach to chronic loss improvement, you are ready to take on the challenge of reaching the zero defect and zero breakdown targets. If this is done thoroughly, those targets can, indeed, be reached.

7

Autonomous Maintenance Activities of the Production Department

One characteristic of TPM is that the production department is required to participate through autonomous maintenance as performed by the equipment operators. This chapter examines its goals and methods.

DEFINITION OF AUTONOMOUS MAINTENANCE

The purpose of autonomous maintenance is to teach equipment operators how to maintain their equipment by performing daily checks, lubrication, replacement of parts, repairs, precision checks, and other maintenance tasks, including the early detection of abnormalities.

Each Operator Is Responsible for Maintaining His or Her Own Equipment

Traditionally, the general thinking among equipment operators has been "I run it, you fix it." Operators considered themselves responsible only for setting up unprocessed workpieces and checking the quality of processed ones. They regarded all maintenance, including light maintenance and lubrication, as the responsibility of maintenance staff. By now it should be obvious that this way of thinking is a mistake. Now and then some operators may deviate from their philosophy to lend a hand in maintenance, but the "I run it, you fix it" attitude is completely wrong.

The consequences are sad indeed, for operators can prevent breakdowns simply by getting a feel for abnormalities through physical contact with the equipment — taking a little time to tighten loose bolts, lubricating dry parts and cleaning away dirt, noticing dirt or grime on friction surfaces, the accumulation of dirt or cutting oil on limit switches — things that shorten equipment life.

While all these are easy enough to do, in very few factories are they done well. Often you can find clogged drains, empty oil supply equipment, and other results of maintenance neglect.

Training Operators to Understand Their Equipment

Autonomous maintenance requires operators to understand their equipment. The job-related expertise must not be limited to simply operating the equipment; it must also include a lot of things traditionally regarded as maintenance work. The need for this approach is becoming increasingly obvious as factories introduce more robots and automated systems. Most of all, equipment operators need to learn how to detect abnormalities. This means acquiring the ability to look at the quality of the products and the performance of the equipment and notice when something is strange.

This depends on the following three skills:

1. A clear understanding of the criteria for judging normal and abnormal conditions (the ability to establish equipment conditions).
2. Strict enforcement of condition management rules (the ability to maintain equipment conditions).
3. A quick response to abnormalities (the ability to repair and restore equipment conditions).

When an operator has mastered all three skills, he or she will understand the equipment well enough to recognize the causes of future problems and realize, "this machine is about to produce defects," or "this machine is about to break down." He or she will also be able to respond quickly. The following list describes some of the skills such operators need.

1. The ability to detect equipment abnormalities and make improvements.

- Ability to watch for and discover abnormalities in equipment operation and components.
- Understanding the importance of proper lubrication, including correct lubrication methods and methods for checking lubrication.

- Understanding the importance of cleaning (inspection) and proper cleaning methods.
- Understanding the importance of localizing scattered cutting debris and coolant, and the ability to make localizing improvements.
- Ability to restore or repair (improve) abnormalities they discover.

2. The ability to understand equipment functions and mechanisms, and the ability to detect causes of abnormalities.

- Understanding what to look for when checking mechanisms.
- Ability to clean and inspect to maintain equipment performance.
- Understanding criteria for judging abnormalities.
- Understanding the relations between specific causes and specific abnormalities.
- Ability to confidently judge when the equipment needs to be shut off.
- Some ability to perform breakdown diagnosis.

3. The ability to understand the relationship between equipment and quality, and the ability to predict problems in quality and detect their causes.

- Ability to physically analyze problem-related phenomena.
- Understanding the relationship between characteristics of quality and the equipment.
- Understanding tolerance ranges for static and dynamic precision, and how to measure such precision.
- Understanding causal factors behind defects.

4. The ability to make repairs.

- Ability to replace parts.
- Understanding life expectancy of parts.
- Ability to deduce causes of breakdowns.

- Ability to take emergency measures.
- Ability to assist in overhaul repairs.

Obviously, anyone who masters all these skills has achieved a very high level indeed, and no one is expected to do that quickly. Instead, each skill should be studied and practiced for whatever time it takes to acquire proficiency.

Figure 7-1 shows how the development of operators who understand their equipment relates to the four steps in autonomous maintenance.

CHARACTERISTICS OF AUTONOMOUS MAINTENANCE DEVELOPMENT

The following is a detailed look at the characteristics and development of an autonomous maintenance program. The

Step	Skills	Relation to autonomous maintenance	Related training	
1.	• Ability to recognize equipment abnormalities • Ability to make improvements	Step 1: Initial cleaning — — — — — — — Step 2: Eliminate sources of contamination and inaccessible areas — — — — — — — Step 3: Creation and maintenance of cleaning and lubrication standards	• Develop an eye for spotting abnormalities • Develop the ability to make improvements that eliminate abnormalities By creating the standards themselves, operators are better able to maintain those standards	TPM introduction-related education	Foremen or their superiors
2.	Understanding of equipment functions and mechanisms	Step 4: General inspection	Experienced operators teach less experienced ones about the proper equipment conditions, equipment functions and structure, and other maintenance-related knowledge.	General inspection studies	Group leaders or department chiefs
3.	Understanding of the relation between quality and equipment conditions	Step 5: Autonomous inspection — — — — — — — Step 6: Workplace organization and housekeeping (workplace management and control) — — — — — — — Step 7: Fully implemented autonomous maintenance program	Organization of data describing defect-free equipment conditions, and maintenance management to maintain those conditions	P-M analysis studies	Department chief, section chief, or group leader
4.	Ability to repair equipment	Small repairs —————— Large repairs	(Learned though maintenance skill courses)	Improvement of maintenance skills	Foremen, PM staff, operators

Figure 7-1. Training Operators to Understand Their Equipment

steps outlined are the creation of my colleague Mr. Fumio Gotoh and are based on his many years of experience as a TPM consultant.

A Step-by-Step Approach

It is very difficult to do several things at the same time. That's why autonomous maintenance training takes a step-by-step approach, making sure each key skill is thoroughly learned before going on to the next. Autonomous maintenance development has been organized into seven steps, and these will be described in detail in the next section of this chapter.

Use of Audits

Autonomous maintenance trainees are given audits to determine whether or not they are ready to go on to the next level (see Figure 7-2).

There are three reasons for these audits:

1. To determine whether or not each level has been fully implemented.
2. To aid small groups by providing feedback from management on the strengths and weaknesses of their autonomous maintenance activities.
3. To make clear what needs to be achieved and how to best achieve it.

Sometimes groups will pass on the first audit and sometimes only after the second or third. But the important thing is to improve the way groups think about their equipment and to lend them support. A characteristic of this program is that audits must be requested. When filling out the request form, the groups describe what problems have taken most of their efforts and what improvements they emphasized (see Figure 7-3).

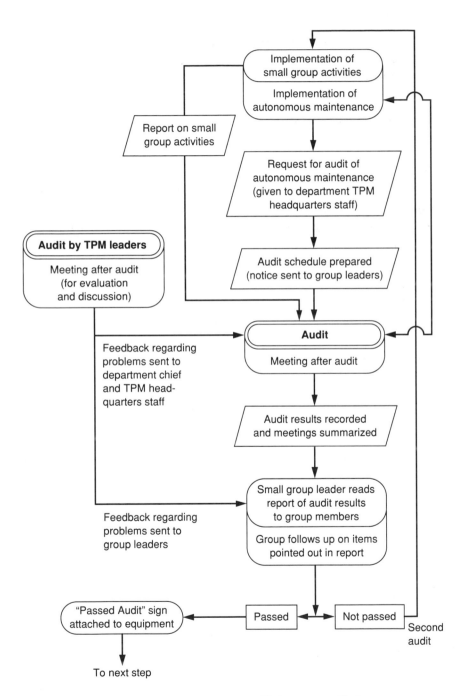

Figure 7-2. Audit Cycle for Autonomous Maintenance Trainees

Audit Request Form

TPM Autonomous Maintenance Audit Request Form

Procedural step to be audited: *Step 1*

	Dept.

To be completed by applicant

Workshop making request	*Bearing factory, Dept. 4 Group 2, Section 1*	Equipment to be audited		
Name of small group	*"Our Gang"*	No. of equipment units to be audited		
Name of leader (No. of people in group)	*Dan Graham, Men: 2 Women: 2 Total: 4*		No. of repeats	Item
Self-evaluation score (date)	*85 points (February 9)*	Activities to date	1	
			2	
Desired audit date	*February 12, about 1:00pm*		3	

Result indicators	*No. of idling and minor stoppage incidents, rework rate, changes in changeover time*

Points of emphasis for audit

1. Group activities (No. of meetings prior to this audit)

Cleaning takes a lot of time because of the large number of machines in our section. We also spent a lot of time discussing ways to locate abnormalities and put a lot of emphasis on discovering them.

2. Workshop audit

We would like to find out if we overlooked any abnormalities. We would also like an evaluation of the improvement we made to localize the scattering of honing fluid.

To be completed by auditors

Audit date/time	*February 12, 1-3 pm*	Audit team meeting place
Audit team members	*McKenzie, Jones & Rodriquez*	

Figure 7-3. Audit Request Form

In one case, a group had failed both the first and second audits. At first the leader was reluctant to attempt a third, since the results of the second pointed out so many things that needed improvement. However, the group members got together and realized they had been taking the wrong approach. They changed their methods, attacked each problem one by one, and were not afraid to get their hands dirty. As they prepared for the third audit, they found new enthusiasm, even coming to work on their days off. When the results came in and they learned they had finally passed, the group members were ecstatic and justly proud of their achievement.

Organization-Led Activities

Although the word *autonomous* implies that small groups perform these activities completely under their own authority, they are much more likely to succeed if, at least in the early stages, they receive guidance from the TPM organization, operating under a chain of authority in which the group leader receives guidance from the foreman, the foreman from the section leader, the section leader from the department manager, and so on.

An important boost is provided when upper-level employees, such as section and department managers, help groups avoid or get out of dead-end pursuits, move along faster, or hold up their strong points as examples for others to follow.

It is much better to avoid having completely autonomous small groups, even in autonomous maintenance development. In this sense the small groups used for autonomous maintenance development are completely different from traditional QC circles, which are highly independent groups. This is because everything done within the framework of autonomous maintenance forms part of the work done within the company organization. In TPM this is called *overlapping small group activities*. In other words, there are shop-floor groups consisting of factory workers and their leaders, middle-management groups consisting of factory section leaders, another group above that, and so on. The higher-level circles check the activities of lower-level groups, while giving them advice to help overcome difficulties or weaknesses.

Use of Activity Boards

Although activity boards are a common tool for most small group activities, they are rarely used effectively and quite often function simply as display boards. Their original purposes are as follows:

- To describe the activities undertaken and to show how far they have progressed so it is easy to see what the group is trying to achieve, by what date, and in what manner.
- To describe the strategy and orientation of the group; that is, their overall concept of their activities and methods.
- To post results of statistical trends for the six big losses (defects, breakdowns, idling and minor stoppages, etc.), overall efficiency, operating time, performance rate, maintenance calls, lubricant consumption, cleaning times, etc. All these should describe the relationship between the group's activities and its accomplishments.
- To describe key issues being emphasized as well as the reasons for immediate actions and an indication of the next key issue to be addressed.
- To record issues to be reviewed, such as breakdowns, discovered causes, overlooked factors, unanswered questions, and plans for the future.
- To describe case studies of improvements and abnormalities discovered, as well as improvement examples from other workshops.
- To list the number of abnormalities found.

By including most, if not all the preceding information, activity boards can describe small group activities in detail. This helps people understand what problems remain. It also helps promote cooperation among different groups and invigorates their activities by showing how they are doing in comparison with other groups.

Students Become Teachers

Any small group leader who has been educated in the basics of TPM is obliged to teach what he or she has learned to other group members. They are encouraged to not only teach what they have learned from TPM classes, but also impart their own experience-based understanding and any "tricks" they have devised for hastening progress. By being a teacher for other group members, they establish themselves as true leaders, and the relationship of teacher to students also brings them into a closer understanding of each other.

After undergoing basic TPM studies, students should be tested, and anyone who scores less than 80 points should be required to repeat the course.

Effective Single-point Lessons

One very effective tool small group leaders can use in teaching other group members is the single-point lesson. This is a lesson focusing on one main point regarding autonomous maintenance, which the teacher organizes and embellishes with drawings. There are three types (see Figures 7-4 through 7-6):

- Basic lessons (use basic information sheet). These present all the basic information group members need to know.
- Problem case study lessons (use problem case study sheet). These describe actual breakdowns, defects, or other problems and teach how their recurrence can be prevented.

- Improvement case study lessons. These explain how certain shop-floor small groups made improvements and what results they achieved.

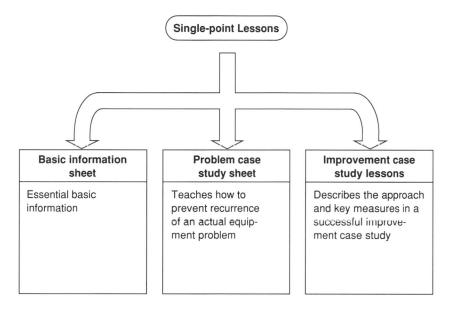

Figure 7-4. Types of Single-point Lessons

Meetings

Enthusiastic meetings attended by all group members are essential for energetic small group activities. In autonomous maintenance development, it is especially important that all members participate, and pool their collective wisdom to work out plans. Small group activities will not work unless everyone feels part of the group. Discussions should not be dominated by one or two people; rather they should always be conducted with a team spirit.

Small group leaders bear the ultimate responsibility for the success or failure of the meetings. Moreover, leaders who

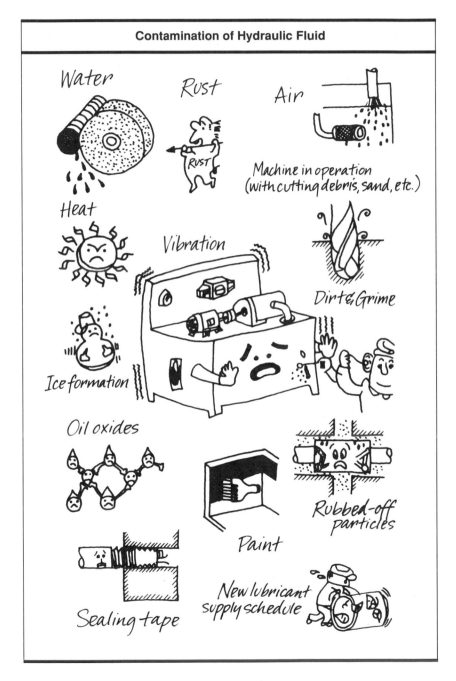

Figure 7-5. Single-point Lesson Case Study No. 1

Hydraulic Device and Contamination

○ *Because the hydraulic device has such narrow internal clearance spaces, it cannot tolerate much contamination and still operate efficiently.*

Example	Section	Specified clearance range (microns)
	Pocket valve	13~40
	Vane pump (vane sides)	5~13
	Valve (spool & sleeve)	1~23
	Gear box (gear wheel & side plate)	0.5~5

• *Contamination is the No. 1 enemy of hydraulic equipment.*

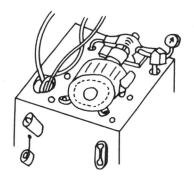

○ *Are any unnecessary holes being left in the equipment?*

○ *Is drain pipe properly inserted into tank?*

○ *Is lid on oil supply hole fastened securely?*

Carry out improvement measures at all locations where contaminants may enter the equipment.

Figure 7-6. Single-point Lesson Case Study No. 2

practice overly strong leadership are just as undesirable as those who provide little or no leadership. They should get members to speak up and emphasize the positive aspects of everyone's opinions. To help meetings go smoothly, leaders should come with a prepared list of topics for discussion — goals, improvement targets, required improvement points, estimations of results, strategies, and problem issues. Finally, leaders should be skilled at bringing themes into sharp focus, limiting discussion time; finding effective ways of discussing, organizing, and summarizing the ideas of members; and listing suggested goals.

Mandatory Reports

The group leader is responsible for ensuring that a report is filled out to record the meeting's contents, the conclusions reached, the next meeting date, and other facts. This should be sent to the department chief (see Figure 7-7).

These reports are submitted so the department chief can keep informed of what the group members are trying to achieve and the problems encountered on the way. In addition, the reports enable group members to receive advice and other feedback from management. It does not matter how complimentary, critical, or detailed the manager's comments are; the important thing is that the group members receive feedback from higher-ups. Any kind will wield a strong influence on the members.

AUTONOMOUS MAINTENANCE DEVELOPMENT STEPS

The seven steps for implementing autonomous maintenance are

Step 1. Initial cleaning
Step 2. Eliminate sources of contamination and inaccessible areas

Group Activities Report	Date issued: *October 18*
	Group name: *Helical Circle*

Theme:	Department: *Third Tool Dept., Group 1, Section 5*
Preparing for the Step 2 audit	Group leader: *Davies* Secretary: *Comarella*

Participants: *Comarella, Skinner, Labelle, Burns, Valdez*	**Activities**	Shop-floor work:
		Meeting: *Oct. 15, 3:50 to 5:00 pm*
		Classroom activities:
Absentees: *None*		Total work-hours: *(1.1 hours) × (5 persons) = 5.5 work-hours*

No.	Item	Description of action or plan	Start date	Done by
1.	*Audit on Step 2 scheduled for Oct. 22. Discussed what needs to be done before then.*	*1) Review initial cleaning (both day & night shifts must devote 15 minutes after the break period to thorough initial cleaning.)*	*Oct. 8*	*All*
		2) Make list of most important items for initial cleaning.	*Oct. 8*	*Labelle*
		3) Post descriptions of oil leakage countermeasures (tagging, etc.) on activities board.	*Oct. 20*	*Valdez*
2.	*Installed cover to localize debris on MC unit, but the unit is not being used now, so the effect of the cover has not been tested yet.*	*1) Use D9 MC to make model for testing effectiveness of improvement.*	*Oct. 20*	*Skinner, Burns*
3.	*Still no progress on improvement of intake port (response to source of problem).*	*1) Experiment with DP MC, keep statistics on grinder powder.*	*Oct. 20*	*Skinner, Burns, Comarella*

Comment by Dept. Chief:	Comment by Dept. TPM Office:	Comment by Factory Group Leader:
Group should read up on Step 3	*Should hold meetings more often*	*Use the PDCA cycle*

Figure 7-7. Group Activities Report

Step 3. Creation and maintenance of cleaning and lubrication standards

Step 4. General inspection

Step 5. Autonomous inspection

Step 6. Workplace organization and housekeeping (workplace management and control)

Step 7. Fully implemented autonomous maintenance program

Although it is generally best to complete all seven steps, in some cases the size of the factory, the types of equipment used, or other factors warrant stopping after Step 5. The scope of this book limits our detailed description to the first five steps as well.

Step 1: Initial Cleaning

In this first step, the group puts the "cleaning is inspecting" motto into practice and confirms it with their own experience.

Initial Cleaning Helps Reveal Abnormalities

The physical act of touching the equipment and shifting it around helps in the discovery of abnormalities. The five senses are used to detect looseness and vibration, wear, misalignment, deflection, abnormal noise, overheating, and oil leaks. In any workshop, cleaning is bound to reveal numerous abnormalities, and many will be the kind that, unless detected early, lead to major equipment defects, breakdowns, and/or product defects (see Figure 7-8).

Sometimes cleaning reveals big surprises, such as a cracked frame that had been masked by accumulated grime, a lubrication inlet also hidden by dirt, or limit switches so covered with grime they no longer function correctly.

Thorough cleaning means taking equipment apart to clean internal parts the operators may never have seen, so this is a kind of inspection that naturally leads to discovering

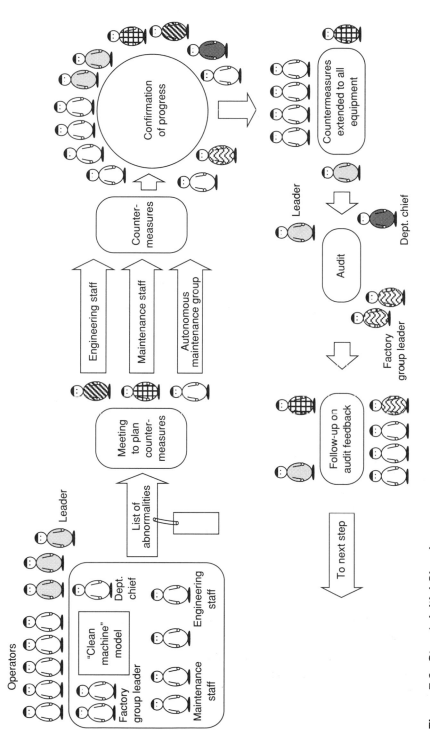

Figure 7-8. Step 1: Initial Cleaning

abnormalities. It is very important that operators performing these tasks are taught the correct way to inspect equipment, look for abnormalities, judge the difference between abnormalities and normal conditions, and look for causes. For example, when cleaning the inside of a hydraulic fluid tank, operators should be taught to look for sludge accumulation and clogged or broken filters — things not ordinarily discovered when operating the equipment.

Find the Source of Contamination

If the equipment becomes dirty soon after cleaning, find the source of contamination. Often a source of dirt or oil leakage will not be visible unless the equipment is thoroughly cleaned at least once a day, and this time-consuming task will itself prompt the operators to look harder for ways to reduce or eliminate contamination. When they start asking themselves why the equipment should continue to leak and how they can prevent it, the seeds for improvement have been planted. When autonomous maintenance is implemented at any company, expect a wealth of experience-based improvements and energetic improvement planning to result.

In workshops where all the equipment is new and is being managed properly, initial cleaning will do little to expose hidden abnormalities. But initial cleaning is still valuable, since it helps the operators better understand how various parts function. They can learn how limit switches operate and how sensor signals correspond to equipment mechanisms. In other words, it gives them a better grasp of the whole series of motions and processes involved in the equipment operation.

When Possible, Operators Should Correct Abnormalities Themselves

Generally, when workshop groups implement the "five S's" — seiri (sorting out), seiton (arranging efficiently), seiso (checking through cleaning), seiketsu (purity), and shitsuke (discipline) — the result is only superficial beautification. Equipment exteriors are restored to a shiny, like-new look, but the hidden interiors are still covered with dirt and grime and full of abnormalities. Since the main purpose is to discover abnormalities, obviously such skin-deep cleaning is insufficient. When the primary goal is to rid the equipment of abnormalities and prevent the scattering of dirt and debris, it will be cleaned as part of the process.

When an operator finds an abnormality, he or she should tag its location. The workshop group then needs to figure out which abnormalities they can correct themselves and which must be looked into by a maintenance technician, and they should set a deadline for correcting each one. Operators should take care of as many as possible by themselves, since this will deepen their concern for their equipment.

Step 2: Eliminate Sources of Contamination and Inaccessible Areas

In this step, make improvements to eliminate contamination and leakage of lubricant, air, or fuel (see Figure 7-9).

Fix the Sources of Contamination

Improvements might consist of repairing a hydraulic fluid pipe joint from which fluid has been leaking or reducing the volume of lubricant to stop an overflow-related leakage. The essential point is that it is necessary to stop the contamination at its source. When this is not possible, like when the source is a blade scattering cutting debris, or if the use of cutting fluid scatters debris and fluid, at least improvements can be made to minimize the dispersion of these contaminants, such as installing shields as close to the source of contamination as possible to localize it.

Improve Areas that Are Inaccessible for Cleaning and Inspection

These include areas that are difficult, impossible, or require a lot of time to clean and check. In this step the group needs to render these areas accessible. For example, if an FRL (filter, regulator, and lubricator) is installed too close to the floor, removing the filter to check the lubricator becomes difficult. In this case, reposition the equipment to facilitate inspection. If there are V-belts that require checking, install a window rather than having to remove a cover to check them. Likewise, simplify the wiring and piping layout whenever possible.

Emphasize the Joy of Making Improvements

In this step it is important that group members not only learn about the need for improvements and the proper meth-

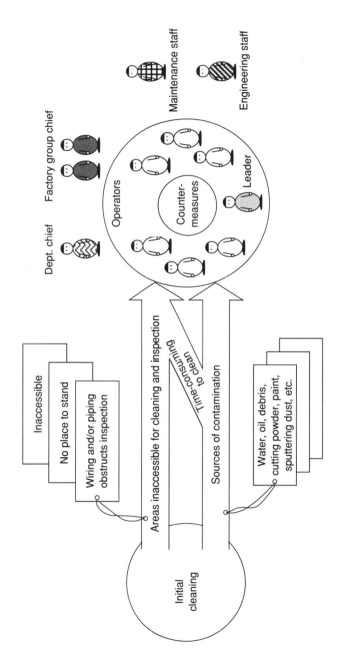

Figure 7-9. Step 2: Eliminate Sources of Contamination and Inaccessible Areas

ods for making them, but also the confidence and joy that can be gained.

When making improvements, group members need to acquire firsthand experience of the trial-and-error process by trying improvements that often fail but eventually lead to hard-won success. Through this experience they learn not to grow despondent over failures but to persist in their improvement goals. After all, it's the hard-won battles that bring the greatest joy of victory. Accordingly, you should encourage improvements to be as "home grown" as possible by allowing them to be initiated and carried out by the groups themselves.

Typical of this approach is when group members put up cardboard shields around sources of scattered cutting debris, run the equipment for a time, then remove them to see what the scattering range is before designing a permanent shield. Often group members localize debris by putting up a large cover that blankets the entire machine. This is not a very good way to make the improvement, since large shields make it difficult to see (inspect) what is going on inside. The cutting oil may run out, and such difficulties can lead to oversights and abnormalities that shorten equipment life.

Summary of improvement points. The following is a list of key points for making improvements:

- Make the equipment easier to clean.
- Minimize the spread of dirt, dust, and grime.
- Stop contamination at its source.
- Minimize the scattering of cutting oil and cutting debris.
- Speed up the flow of cutting oil to prevent the accumulation of cutting debris.
- Minimize the area through which cutting oil flows.
- Make the equipment easier to inspect.
- Install inspection windows in the equipment.
- Tighten loose areas in the equipment.
- Eliminate the need for oil pans.
- Install more oil gauges.

- Change the locations of the lubrication inlets.
- Change the lubrication method.
- Rationalize the wiring layout.
- Change the piping layout.
- Make it easier to replace equipment parts.

Step 3: Creation and Maintenance of (Provisional) Standards for Cleaning and Lubrication

In this step, group members use their experiences from the first two to determine the optimal cleaning and lubrication conditions for their equipment and to draft preliminary work standards for its maintenance (see Figure 7-10). Work standards specify what needs to be done, where, the reason, methods, and time frame. To do all this they must decide which parts of the equipment need cleaning every day, which methods to use, how to inspect the equipment, judge abnormalities, and so on. Having these standards will help them carry out their cleaning tasks with greater confidence and ability.

Group Members Should Set Their Own Standards

Having accepted responsibility for their equipment, group members should decide by themselves how they are going to maintain it. When it comes to cleaning and lubrication standards, many workshops have already established them. But very few follow them thoroughly, mainly because the people who set the standards are often not the ones who must follow them. To help set cleaning and lubrication standards likely to be followed, three criteria may be used:

1. The people *doing* the cleaning and lubricating need to understand the vital importance of these tasks.
2. The equipment must be improved to facilitate cleaning and lubrication.
3. The time required for cleaning and lubrication must be an official part of the daily schedule.

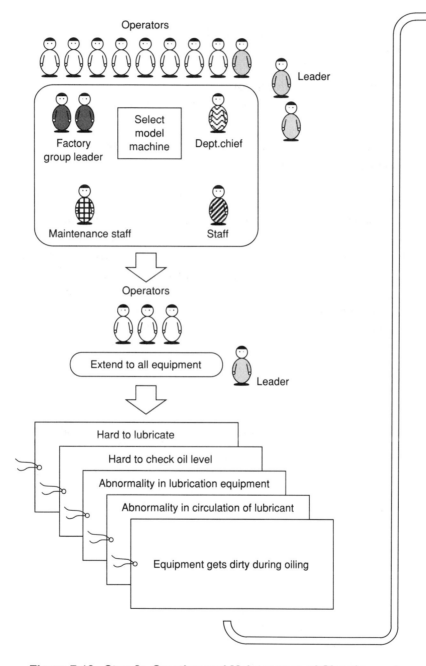

Figure 7-10. Step 3: Creation and Maintenance of Cleaning and Lubrication Standards

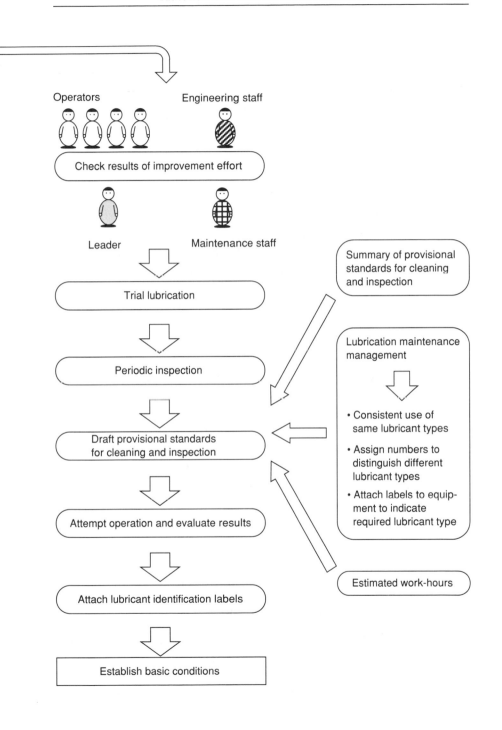

Cleaning and lubrication standards will not be followed unless everyone in the group understands — theoretically and practically — why these are so important. But the time given to cleaning and lubrication cannot be unlimited; neither can it be undefined. If the duration of these activities is not kept within certain limits, it will add up to a great amount of time. To keep cleaning and lubrication times short, group members need to devise time-saving improvements, and unless these are made, time constraints will result in either substandard performance of maintenance tasks or their complete omission.

The work done in Steps 1 and 2 has prepared the group to set standards for cleaning and inspection, the methods and criteria to be used, responses to be made, time allowed, and the schedule of periodic maintenance. When doing this, the group must measure the time required for each task and devise ways to shorten the duration of the more time-consuming ones. They also need to schedule daily and weekly maintenance and avoid imbalances by reorganizing the tasks or making time-saving improvements. Overall, the hours spent on cleaning and lubrication should not exceed 2 percent of the total work-hours.

It is also important to incorporate the lessons learned from sporadic breakdowns or defects. Even when a breakdown is inevitable, you can still find its causes, devise better ways to inspect for abnormalities, and prevent it from recurring. This information must be incorporated into the cleaning and inspection standards in order to improve those standards.

Figure 7-11 summarizes cleaning and lubrication standards.

Key Points for Creating Lubrication Standards

Keep the following points in mind:

- Clearly specify the lubricant to be used, and unify types whenever possible to reduce variety and promote consistency.
- Thoroughly list all lubrication inlets and other sites.

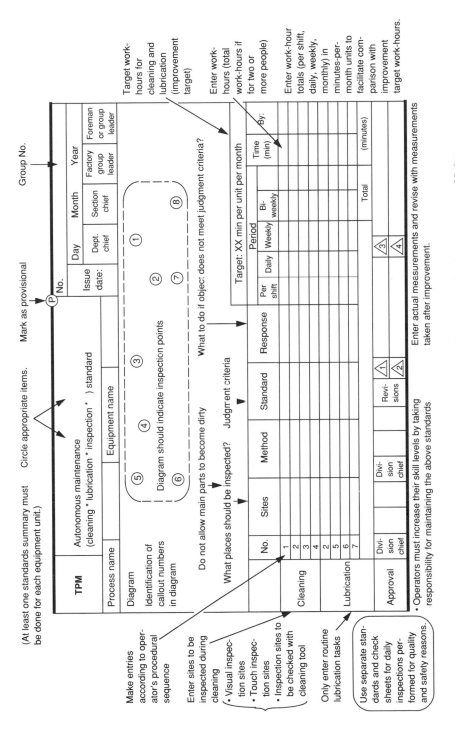

Figure 7-11. Summary of Provisional Cleaning and Lubrication Standards for Autonomous Maintenance

- In centrally lubricated equipment, improve the lubrication system and diagram it (see Figure 7-12) showing the route from pump to main pipes, branch valves, branch pipes, and lubrication points.
- Check for blockage in branch valves and differences in branched volumes, and find out if lubricant is reaching all lubrication points.
- Measure the lubricant consumption rate (during one day or one week).
- Measure the amount used per application.
- Measure the pipe lengths (especially grease pipes) to see, for example, if two pipes may be needed instead of one.
- Review the disposal method for dirty lubricant (after greasing).
- Create lubrication labels and attach them to all lubrication points.
- Establish a service station (for maintenance of lubricants and lubrication equipment).
- List all difficulties concerning lubrication.
- Work out the division of lubrication-related responsibilities with the maintenance department.

Step 4: General Inspection

For operators to understand their equipment, they must be instructed in the common aspects of different types, as well as the peculiarities of each unit (see Figure 7-13).

Understanding the Basic Technologies

In this fourth step, operators receive basic instruction in lubrication, equipment parts (tightening nuts and bolts), pneumatics, hydraulics, electrical circuits, drive systems, and other basic technologies such as waterproofing and fire prevention, in

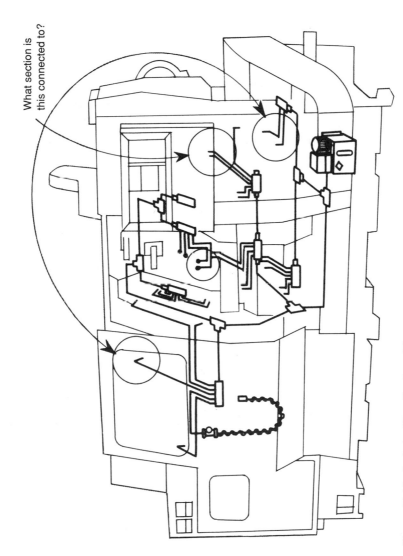

What section is this connected to?

Figure 7-12. Lubrication System Diagram

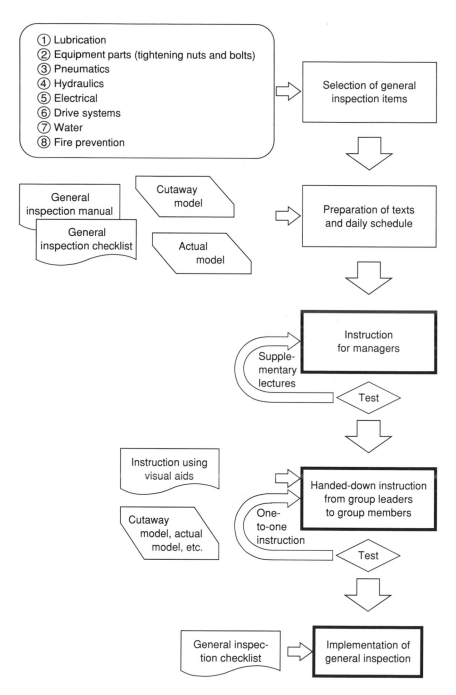

Figure 7-13. Step 4: General Inspection

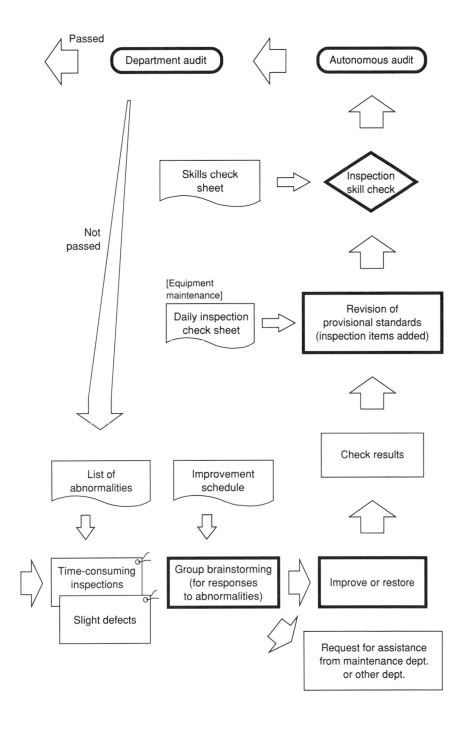

order to use this knowledge while inspecting their equipment and watching for abnormalities.

In pneumatics, for example, operators need to understand the functions and structure of FRLs (filter, regulator, and lubricator sets) and how to adjust the volume of lubricant. This is valuable when cleaning and checking pneumatic equipment. Such training enables operators to perform inspections knowing the particular points they must check and the most important maintenance management points.

Procedure for Step 4

Carry out Step 4 as follows:

- Basic training (class for leaders)
- Handed-down training (leaders teach group members)
- Operators put training into practice to find abnormalities
- Promotion of visual control

Basic training in equipment skills. The technical staff and maintenance specialists can use text materials, cutaway models, and samples for teaching basic maintenance to equipment operators. Specifically, they should teach the structure of the equipment, its functions, proper adjustments and use, structural problem points, and daily checkpoints. This is taught in Step 4 because it carries on from the first three steps, making this the most effective time to learn about equipment, abnormalities, and the positive results to be gained through patient efforts at making improvements.

If students were not already familiar with the equipment, these lessons in basic maintenance would not have nearly the same effectiveness. Up to this point, methods for discovering abnormalities have been limited to using the five senses. Now it is time to teach the operators how an understanding of the structure and functioning of the equipment will enable them to discover abnormalities using logical analysis.

Consider the simple example of a bolt. The operator can use his common sense to tell if the bolt is tight, but he must be trained to know that it is properly tightened only when the correct amount of torque has been used. For example, to achieve 50,000 psi bolt stress, a 1-inch lubricated flange bolt requires a final torque value of 350 ft-lbs. To apply the correct torque rating to make best use of the bolt, you apply not only common sense but also theoretical knowledge.

Handed-down training (leaders teach group members). When group leaders hand their training down to group members, they should not simply repeat what they have learned. Before teaching the group they should incorporate ideas of their own and make the lessons relate directly to the needs of the particular workshop and its equipment. Obviously the group leader cannot teach something he or she does not understand well. But as the leader brushes up on this knowledge, he or she takes firm possession of the subject and becomes more aware of the leadership role. In attempting to teach the material the leader may find points about which he or she is still uncertain, so consultation with technicians and maintenance staff should be repeated to improve the level of understanding. Likewise, the leader should test students to see if they really understand what they have been taught, if they can put the lessons into practice — actually discovering abnormalities. After all, it is not uncommon for teachers to finish a lesson before their students have understood it, or for students to imagine they have understood something when they have not. The group leader should test the students and retest all who do not pass until they do. The group members will feel a lot better about their autonomous inspection work when they realize their mistakes or see where they had been too lenient in enforcing standards.

Operators put training into practice to find abnormalities. To make sure they have learned more than just intellectual knowledge, equipment operators must discover its true value by practicing it. They should do this as soon as possible, to experience firsthand what it's like to find abnormalities using their newly acquired knowledge.

It's also important to incorporate each checkpoint introduced during the lessons into the provisional standards manual as standard checkpoints.

Promotion of visual control. As the term *visual control* suggests, these are visual cues or indicators used to check equipment or find abnormalities. They should be obvious enough for anyone to see and understand, and in promoting their use the following points should be emphasized:

- What is the object to be checked?
- What is the proper (optimal) condition of that object?
- How should that condition be maintained?
- Does the operator understand the function and structure of the equipment?
- Does the operator understand the proper checking method and criteria for judging abnormalities?
- Does the operator understand how to treat various problems?

One common practice for visual control is placing match marks on all the bolts. Having understood the function of each nut and bolt pair, operators tighten the bolts to their specified torque and then mark them with match marks. However, distinctions should be made among certain bolts. Blade adjustment bolts may require autonomous maintenance. Bolts for which tightness is particularly critical must be prevented from loosening, and only after those measures are taken should they be given match marks. In other words, certain rules must be established to govern full implementation of each maintenance task.

The following list provides some ideas for visual controls of various autonomous maintenance activities (see Figure 7-14).

Lubrication

- Color-coded marks to indicate oil inlets
- Oil level and supply period labels
- Indication of upper and lower oil level limits
- Indication of oil consumption per standard time unit
- Color-coded marks on oil cans to indicate oil types

Equipment parts (tightening nuts and bolts)

- "Inspected" marks and match marks
- Color-coding (blue dots) on bolts for maintenance purposes
- Color-coded (yellow) marks for inlets that do not require bolting (i.e., unused inlets)

Pneumatics

- Pneumatic pressure gauge
- Oil level display
- Display of upper and lower oil level limits
- Solenoid application label
- Tube connection marks (INLET, OUTLET)

Hydraulics

- Hydraulic pressure gauge
- Oil level display
- Oil type display
- Thermo label for hydraulic pump
- Solenoid application label
- Locknut match marks on relief valve

Drive systems

- Display of V-belt/chain type
- Display of V-belt/chain direction of rotation
- Install peep window for checking belts

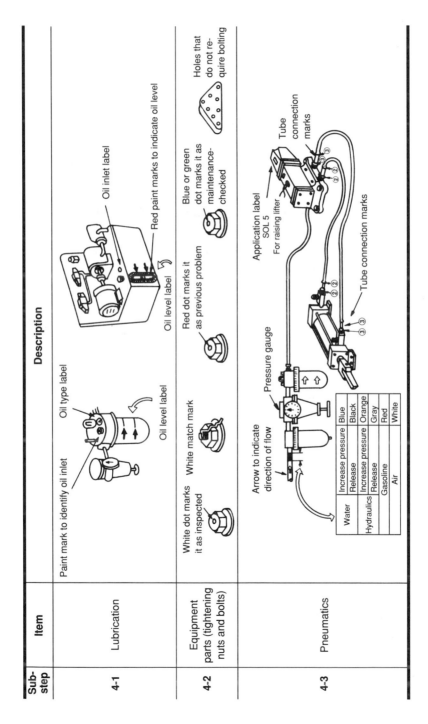

Sub-step	Item	Description
4-1	Lubrication	Paint mark to identify oil inlet / Oil type label / Oil level label / Oil inlet label / Red paint marks to indicate oil level / Oil level label / White dot marks it as inspected / Holes that do not require bolting
4-2	Equipment parts (tightening nuts and bolts)	White match mark / Red dot marks it as previous problem / Blue or green dot marks it as maintenance-checked
4-3	Pneumatics	Arrow to indicate direction of flow / Pressure gauge / Application label SOL 5 For raising lifter / Tube connection marks / Tube connection marks

Water — Increase pressure — Blue
Release — Black
Hydraulics — Increase pressure — Orange
Release — Gray
Gasoline — Red
Air — White

Figure 7-14. Example of Visual Control

Step 5: Autonomous Inspection

In this step, create and enforce basic standards by combining the provisional standards created in Step 3 with the additional check items for daily general inspection (see Figure 7-15).

After listing all inspection items for each piece of equipment split the list into two: items that can be handled using autonomous inspection and items requiring inspection by maintenance specialists.

If any sporadic breakdowns have occurred, operators should work with the maintenance staff to develop inspection points that prevent the breakdown from happening again and that can be performed as part of autonomous inspection. Next, these new inspection points must be incorporated into the standards.

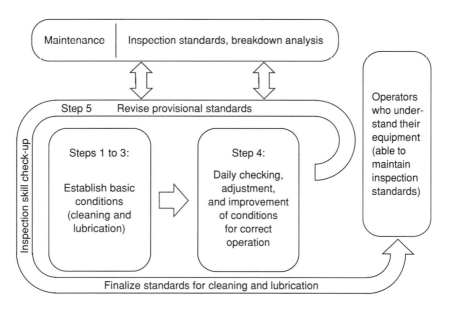

Figure 7-15. Step 5: Autonomous Inspection

At this step the activities are as follows:

- Review the item, method, and time standards for cleaning, checking, and lubrication.
- Consult with the maintenance department about inspection points, and make specific and clear job assignments to avoid omissions.
- Check whether or not the inspection tasks can be done within scheduled work-hours, and make time-saving improvements if necessary.
- Check to see if the inspection skill level can be raised.
- Make sure autonomous inspection is carried out correctly by all operators.

In conclusion, no matter how well you make individual improvements that establish the conditions for zero breakdowns and zero defects, unless you enforce a schedule of daily inspection, lubrication, and precision checks, breakdowns and defects will return. In other words, how well autonomous inspection is performed determines how permanent the improvements will be. That is why you cannot afford to neglect autonomous inspection and especially cannot neglect the need to cultivate operators who understand their equipment.

8

Planned Maintenance Activities of the Maintenance Department

Chapter 7 discussed autonomous maintenance as carried out by the production department. This chapter looks at more specialized activities for reducing breakdowns and defects performed by professionals in the maintenance department.

Planned maintenance is essential for efficient maintenance activities. This means the performance of maintenance activities according to a specified plan or schedule.

DIVISION OF TASKS BETWEEN MAINTENANCE AND PRODUCTION DEPARTMENTS

Autonomous maintenance activities must be kept within certain limits. For example, the following inspection and measurement activities are beyond the scope of autonomous maintenance as performed by production department workers:

- Tasks requiring special skills
- Overhaul repair in which deterioration is not visible from the outside

129

- Repairs to equipment that is hard to disassemble and reassemble
- Tasks requiring special measurements
- Tasks posing substantial safety risks, such as working in high places

The maintenance department should handle all these tasks and also periodically check to ensure that nothing has been overlooked in the inspection work done by the production department. In all too many factories maintenance staff are too busy responding to sporadic breakdowns and do not have time to carry out periodic and overhaul (disassembly) inspections, so breakdowns continue in the absence of preventive measures. In other words, the greater the number of breakdowns, the less time there is for planned maintenance, and the whole situation works against the possibility of ever reducing that number.

Obviously, neither autonomous nor planned maintenance can succeed, by itself, in reducing breakdowns and defects. Instead, these activities must work together like the two axles of an automobile, and each situation must be studied to see how one can support the other. The maintenance department should cooperate by giving advice for autonomous maintenance and promptly responding to the production department's request to treat abnormalities. When autonomous maintenance progresses to a certain point, it is time to review the division of labor and determine whether the production department is ready to perform tasks that until then had been the responsibility of maintenance. For each type of equipment the maintenance professionals should determine how much cleaning, inspection, repair, and parts replacement should be done by the production department and how much requires their more specialized skills. As the level of maintenance skills in the production department rises, more maintenance tasks can be incorporated into its autonomous maintenance activities (see Figure 8-1).

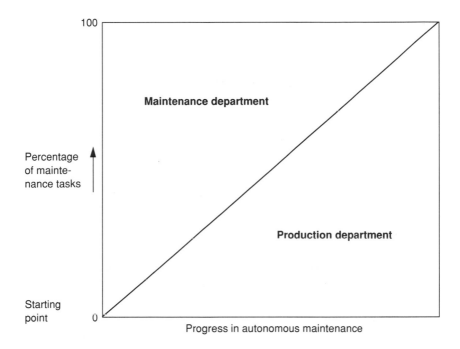

Figure 8-1. Division of Maintenance Tasks between Production and Maintenance Departments

As the maintenance department gradually passes more work to production, their extra work-hours can be directed toward improvement-related maintenance activities. At one company this transition was so successful that it managed to transfer all maintenance activities for its 800-ton class injection molding equipment — including breakdown repairs, pipe laying, oil changes, and disassembly repair of the high-pressure pump — to the production department.

DESCRIPTION OF PLANNED MAINTENANCE ACTIVITIES

The following activities are considered part of planned maintenance.

A Quick Response System

The maintenance department must respond quickly to abnormalities discovered through autonomous maintenance. One reason for doing so is that ignoring them for any length of time lowers the morale of the production workers who took the trouble to point them out.

By the same token, they deserve an explanation when the problems cannot be fixed immediately due to technical difficulties or cost considerations. When no obstacles exist, the maintenance department should fix the problems right away and, to raise the skill levels of the operators, take the opportunity to teach them about the response being taken.

When responding to daily breakdowns, the maintenance people need to work closely with group leaders in the production department, not only by taking emergency measures but by confirming the abnormal phenomena, checking for prior symptoms, searching for causes, checking results of the measures, determining whether or not the same problem is likely to occur in similar equipment, and planning preventions. If possible, they should look into all these things the same day the abnormality occurs.

This cooperation between maintenance and the production leaders is important for the following reasons:

1. It helps production leaders take responsibility for breakdowns in their equipment, shows them what symptoms show up prior to certain breakdowns, teaches them how to respond, and gains their cooperation in taking preventive measures against future breakdowns.
2. It also helps maintenance people improve their own skills by providing opportunities to check the quality of their work, better understand the causes of breakdowns, and learn how to plan preventive measures.

Activities Aimed at Early Discovery of Abnormalities

There are two methods aimed at the early discovery of abnormalities: time-based maintenance (periodic maintenance) and condition-based maintenance (predictive maintenance).

Time-Based Maintenance (Periodic Maintenance)

Time-based maintenance is maintenance performed according to a schedule. It is used for the following activities:

- Periodic inspection (weekly, monthly, yearly)
- Periodic parts replacement
- Periodic overhauls
- Periodic precision measurement (static and dynamic precision)
- Electrostatic oil treatment and oil replacement

Use of maintenance calendars. When there are many equipment units and inspection points to deal with, it is easy to forget when each unit and point was last checked. Maintenance calendars help prevent such problems and should contain a complete listing of the scheduled times for inspections, overhauls, oil changes, parts replacement, and other tasks for each equipment unit. If possible, all should be entered on the same schedule sheet to make the entire range of maintenance activities plainly visible. Generally, these calendars are drawn up in a weekly, monthly, or yearly format. To make the work more effective, a set of inspection and disassembly maintenance standards must also be prepared (see Figure 8-2). Shutting down the equipment at regular intervals for planned, periodic inspection is fundamental for good maintenance.

Fill in one:　○ In planning　● Completed

Annual Maintenance Calendar for 1984

No. 3 Production Dept., Logic Processing Line

Created on:　Day　Month　Year　By: *NAME, No. 3 Production Dept.*　Dept. chief　Group leader

Machine no.	Equipment name	Inspection point	Work-hours	Person responsible	Jan	Feb	Mar	Apr	May	Jun	Jul	Aug	Sep
18038	Internal lathe	1) Check centering on table top	6 mos. 16'	Hubert, Kotze		●						○	
		2) Check vertical vibration in main spindle head and angle of bed glide plane.	20'										
		3) Check spindle vibration	3 mos. 5'										
		4) Check insulation resistance	6 mos. 5'										
		5) Check resistance	6 mos. 30'										

Monthly Periodic Inspection Schedule

April

Equipment name	Equipment no.	Inspection or adjustment	Person responsible	Schedule 1	2	3	4
Grinder	20177	Disassemble table lathe		①			
NC turret miller	16222	Periodic inspection			◤		
NC turret miller	20142	Replace Z-axis thrust bearing				◤	
Machining center	22064	Replace DC spindle motor					◤

Figure 8-2. Annual and Monthly Periodic Maintenance Calendars

Condition-Based Maintenance (Predictive Maintenance)

Condition-based maintenance uses diagnostic devices to measure equipment deterioration or discover abnormalities and their symptoms. It also includes other maintenance performed in response to equipment conditions. Usually some continual monitoring or periodic measuring should be done to track changes in abnormal conditions over time.

The two diagnostic methods used for this kind of predictive maintenance are simple analysis and precision diagnosis.

Simple analysis includes measurements made with a simple vibration gauge such as a machine checker, shock pulse meter, etc., to determine if abnormalities exist. All simple analysis should be set up so that factory-floor equipment operators are able to handle it.

Precision diagnosis, on the other hand, uses tools such as high-precision gauges to discover the sources of vibration and to measure and analyze their frequencies.

The goals of condition-based maintenance are as follows:

- To estimate where abnormalities will occur without disassembling the equipment.
- To permit quality checks of the repairs already made to overhauled equipment.
- To permit estimation of repair periods.
- To reduce maintenance costs by eliminating periodic overhauls.

Activities to Prevent Recurring Breakdowns

Activities to prevent recurring breakdowns make up a large part of breakdown-reduction activities. The following two preventions are particularly important.

1. Individual Improvements to Reduce Chronic Breakdowns

When dealing with chronic breakdowns, the maintenance staff should use its specialized skills to identify weak points in the equipment and help plan and implement improvements.

2. Individual Improvements to Extend Equipment Life

Such improvements include studying materials used for parts with the aim of finding the most durable, selecting better parts, and studying alternative systems and mechanisms.

Activities to Shorten Repair Times

The following activities can function to shorten repair time.

Study of Breakdown Diagnosis

When a breakdown occurs, the time required for repairing it will be much shorter if the machine is equipped with self-diagnostic functions. Usually much of the time between the occurrence of the breakdown and completion of the repair is spent looking for the broken part or parts. Obviously, maintenance people should study the design of self-diagnostic devices and understand how they work. There is a wide assortment on the market, and many are quite expensive. However, the best devices are generally the simple, inexpensive ones that maintenance staff invent themselves to suit their particular situations.

Study Parts Replacement Methods

Maintenance workers can shorten their maintenance and repair hours by replacing parts in subassembled sets, rather than piece by piece. They can also make sure the equipment is set up for external changeover and use subassembly sets for fixing breakdowns and doing routine repairs.

Spare Parts Management

This means organizing spare parts so the right ones are always in the right place at the right time. This should include reducing the variety of parts by finding out which are necessary and which are not, and which can be used in common by different departments.

Other Activities

The following are other activities of the maintenance department.

Lubrication Management

This includes the selection and standardization of lubricants and greases, lubricant analysis, and other activities that facilitate basic lubrication policies, approaches, and management issues.

Documentation Management

The maintenance department should establish a documentation system whereby any chart, specifications list, or manual can be easily retrieved at any time. It should also review its approach to inventories of drawings and its policy on how they are checked and revised.

System for Collecting and Using Maintenance-Related Information

An information system is fundamental for good maintenance because it provides valuable data on equipment improvements, breakdowns, breakdown analysis, and other maintenance-related topics. The maintenance department should develop an information system that enables prompt retrieval and analysis of the history of equipment improvements and breakdowns, MTBF (mean time between failures) data, and other maintenance statistics.

SKILLS TRAINING

The following skill-related conditions are absolutely necessary for successful TPM:

- Equipment operators should possess the training and skills to carry out autonomous maintenance and understand their own equipment.

- Maintenance department staff should possess the training and skills to carry out maintenance and repairs and to smoothly implement preventive maintenance.

More specifically, equipment operators cannot clean and lubricate properly unless they know the tightness of the bolts as well as the structure, functions, and inspection methods for each piece of equipment. And this cannot be merely theoretical knowledge — the operators must be skilled in applying it in cleaning and lubrication. In addition, maintenance staff need to have the skills to make repairs like fitting and replacing keys and bearings. This is why skills training is so important for TPM activities.

Everyone Should Learn the Same Skills

At most companies the maintenance staff consists of people at various skill levels, and there is no training system to raise levels of less-trained technicians other than having them watch better-trained staff at work. Often this results in having some staff working with no understanding of even basic things.

When a breakdown occurs, workers usually call the same maintenance technician that fixed the last one, because they know he or she has the skills to fix it. This is not the way it should be. All maintenance workers should be trained in the same skills and be able to make the same repairs.

Table 8-1 lists the standard curriculum in maintenance staff training courses offered by JIPM.

MP DESIGN AND EARLY EQUIPMENT MANAGEMENT

MP design and early equipment management are two methods of making improvements at the earliest possible stage, with the goal of developing maintenance-free equipment.

Table 8-1. Skill Training Curriculum for Maintenance Staff

Topic	Goal	Day 1	Day 2	Day 3
Unit 1: Tightening nuts and bolts	Ability to read diagrams, understand material characteristics, properly use tools, tighten equipment parts, and adjust their positions. Ability to understand and practice basic "tightening nuts and bolts" operations to maintain the configuration and performance of mechanical drive systems, gears, and transmissions.	1) Orientation 2) Survey 3) How to read drawings 4) How to properly use tools 5) Understanding machine materials 6) How to make match-marks	7) Drilling and boring 8) Tapping 9) Bolt torque tightening 10) Bolt fastening 11) Bolt removal 12) Review	13) Importance of equipment maintenance 14) Review of torque tightening 15) Review and test, followed by report
Unit 2: Keys	Gears, pulleys, sprockets, couplings, etc. To understand the types and characteristics of keys as an important element for fastening shafts and hubs.	1) Review Unit 1 and answer questions 2) Fits and tolerances 3) Filing principles and techniques 4) Types of keys 5) How to file round bars	6) Key types and nomenclature 7) How to install different types of keys 8) How to remove different types of keys 9) Review	10) Review of key fitting 11) Shrink-fitting techniques 12) Review of Unit 2 and test, followed by report

Topic	Goal	Day 1	Day 2	Day 3

Unit 3: **Maintenance** **of spindles** **and bearings**	Abnormalities are rarely caused by spindles themselves, but are instead caused by improper fitting of spindles to gears or pulleys. This unit focuses on repairs to connections, developing knowledge and techniques for anti-friction bearings, recording of vibration and heat data for the equipment being tested, and self-evaluation skills.	1) Review Unit 2 and answer questions
		
		2) Types of spindles and shafts
		
		3) Lubrication
		
		4) Practice in fitting spindles
		
		5) Practice in assembly of spindle bearings
		  (1) Slide bearings
		  (2) Anti-friction
		    bearings
			6) Anti-friction bearing setup
			
			7) Testing and data recording for anti-friction bearings (alignment, lubrication, vibration, temperature)
				8) Lubrication of anti-friction bearings
				
				9) Repair and testing of anti-friction bearings
				
				10) Review of Unit 3 and test, followed by report

Unit 4: **Power trans-** **missions** **(gears,** **belts, and** **chains)**	Apply the lessons from Unit 3 to fastening and alignment methods for gears, belts, and chains as well as chain tightening methods. Learn and practice maintenance skills for all mechanical power transmissions.	1) Review Unit 3 and answer questions
		
		2) Gears
		  (1) Gear types
		  (2) Gear damage and
		    maintenance
			3) Testing gear sets
			
			4) Chain-driven devices
			
			5) Coupling and chain alignment (review)
			
			6) Chain tension adjust-ment devices
			
			7) Testing chain-driven devices
				8) Knowledge and skills for V belt-driven devices
				
				9) Review of Unit 4 and test, followed by report

MP Design

MP (maintenance prevention) design means those activities aimed at preventing breakdowns and defects in newly installed equipment by applying preventive maintenance techniques during the design process. In other words, MP design includes discovering weak points in currently used equipment and giving feedback data to the design engineers. It also includes raising equipment reliability, the design of maintenance-free equipment being the ultimate goal.

The search for weak points in equipment can be carried out from the following perspectives:

Facilitating Autonomous Maintenance

- Can cleaning and inspection be easier?
- Can lubricating be centralized so lubricant is supplied at just one or two inlets per equipment unit?
- Can the piping layout be rationalized, such as by improving the position of FRLs and solenoid devices?
- Can the length and layout of wires be improved?
- Is cutting debris, coolant, etc., scattered around?
- Can the recovery of cutting debris be simplified?

Increasing Ease of Operation

- Can equipment be more resistant to operator errors, such as by changing the positions of switches and the layout of buttons on control panels?
- Can changeover procedure be simplified?
- Can standards be clarified to facilitate adjustments, or can measurement methods be made easier?

Improving Quality

- Have the precision settings and methods been determined (what to measure, how to measure it, limit values, etc.)?
- Are passive precision conditions easy to measure?
- Are active precision conditions easy to measure?
- Is diagnostic equipment easy to set up? Does it have visual displays?

Improving Maintainability

- Have equipment life data been collected, and is work in progress to extend equipment life?
- Can parts replacement be simplified?
- Can replacements be done in preassembled units?
- Are breakdown analysis and repair measures applied to prevention measures in similar equipment?
- Are self-diagnostic functions built into the equipment?
- Can oil supply and oil changing be simplified?

Safety

- Are interlocking methods safe?
- Have safety fences been built around hazardous equipment?

Both the factory-floor people and maintenance staff should give feedback on these matters to the design department so it can incorporate maintenance-preventive improvements into the equipment. Naturally some improvements cost more than others, and equipment design engineers must weigh the cost of each suggestion against the estimated savings.

LCC (Life Cycle Costing)

LCC is an analytical method that considers both the initial (acquisition) and running (maintenance) costs of equipment to calculate the most economical designs. For example, if a certain type has low initial cost but high running costs, the overall (life cycle) costs will be high, resulting in economic losses. High running costs can be caused by frequent breakdowns and rework requiring a lot of maintenance, so this is just another case of being "penny wise and pound foolish." LCC is intended to help avoid the purchase of cheaper equipment that will only cost more in heavy maintenance.

Early Equipment Management

Early equipment management means minimizing the time to achieve stable operation (no breakdowns and minimal defects) during the installation, test-run, and handover (commissioning control) periods. Naturally, to have equipment operating flawlessly at installation would be best, but this is rare, mainly because at least one of the following conditions appears:

- Problems occur that originated at the design stage, such as a poor selection of materials, insufficient strength, etc.
- Problems occur that originated at the fabrication stage, such as incorrect parts dimensions, assembly errors, etc.
- Problems occur that originated during installation and test run, such as insufficient operation levels, installation errors, etc.

The purpose of early equipment management is to discover these problems (or the seeds of such problems) and make improvements to eliminate them. This requires techniques for discovering and responding to predicted problems as well as actual ones at each stage of the process — design planning, chart drafting, fabricating equipment, installing it, and performing operational tests. The key technique for finding such problems was discussed in Chapter 6: making thorough lists of slight defects and lists of systematically predicted causes of problems.

Generally, people notice very few problems in equipment during the design and chart-drafting stages. However, when problems occur at later stages of development, the cost of responding to them is usually higher. Therefore it saves money to tackle problems right from the planning and design stage. During installation and test runs, various debugging methods can discover problems, and these help bring initial hidden defects to the surface. Popular debugging methods include accelerated operation, overload tests, and others that put the equipment under extra severe conditions.

This chapter has shown just how broad the scope of maintenance activities should be, and how careful planning is important to prevent oversights and omissions and to ensure effective maintenance. To smooth the ride on the road to "zero breakdowns" and "zero defects," the two axles of the vehicle — autonomous maintenance and maintenance department activities — must work in close cooperation.

Afterword

Although this book certainly fails to explain TPM completely, I am confident it will help workshop leaders and others gain a good understanding of what TPM is all about.

There are three aspects of TPM I sought to emphasize: its goals, the elimination of chronic loss, and autonomous maintenance.

My most succinct definition is that TPM is a set of activities for restoring equipment to its optimal conditions and changing the work environment to maintain those conditions.

When the TPM philosophy is understood and thoroughly implemented, you can expect truly amazing results. I encourage every reader to follow the three-stage path of "changing the equipment, changing human behavior, and changing the work environment" — and thereby bring new vigor and strength to the workplace.

About the Author

Kunio Shirose graduated with a degree in applied chemistry from Hokkaido University in 1957 and joined the Japan Management Association in 1960. In 1984 he joined the staff of the Japan Institute for Plant Maintenance (JIPM), and in 1988 became a director at JIPM. In 1991 he was promoted to executive vice president of JIPM as well as assistant director of its TPM operations division.

He serves as TPM adviser to many companies in Japan, and his consulting work focuses on improving quality control in human-machine systems and increasing equipment efficiency. He is a member of the PM Prize committee, and has coauthored several books on the subject of TPM.

BOOKS FROM PRODUCTIVITY PRESS

Productivity Press provides individuals and companies with materials they need to achieve excellence in quality, productivity and the creative involvement of all employees. Through sets of learning tools and techniques, Productivity supports continuous improvement as a vision, and as a strategy. Many of our leading-edge products are direct source materials translated into English for the first time from industrial leaders around the world. Call toll-free 1-800-394-6868 for our free catalog.

Uptime
Strategies for Excellence in Maintenance Management
John Dixon Campbell

Campbell outlines a blueprint for a world class maintenance a program by examining, piece by piece, its essential elements leadership (strategy and management), control (data management, measures, tactics, planning and scheduling), continuous improvement (RCM and TPM), and quantum leaps (process reengineering). He explains each element in detail, using simple language and practical examples from a side range of industries. This book is for every manager who needs to see the "big picture" of maintenance management. In addition to maintenance, engineering, and manufacturing managers, all business managers will benefit from this comprehensive yet realistic approach to improving asset performance.
ISBN 1-56327-053-6 / 180 pages / $35.00 / Order UP-B220

Implementing TPM
The North American Experience
Charles J. Robinson and Andrew P. Ginder

The authors documents an approach to TPM planning and deployment that modifies the JIPM 12 step process in order to accommodate the experiences of North American plants. They include details and advice on specific deployment steps, OEE calculation methodology, and autonomous maintenance deployment. They provide detailed step-by-step descriptions of how to make TPM work on the plant floor with a discussion on how to position TPM as supportive and complimentary to all other strategic initiatives a plant may be asked to implement.
1-56327-087-0 / est. 250 pages / $45.00 / Order IMPTPM-220

PRODUCTIVITY PRESS, INC., DEPT. BK, P.O. BOX 13390, PORTLAND, OR 97213-0390
Telephone: 1-800-394-6868   Fax: 1-800-394-6286

P-M Analysis
An Advanced Step in TPM Implementation
Kunio Shirose, Yoshifumi Kimura, and Mitsugu Kaneda

P-M analysis is an effective methodology for finding and controlling the causes of equipment-related chronic losses. Chronic loss stems from complex and interrelated causes and in most cases it is very difficult to know how any single cause impacts the overall problem. P-M Analysis is meant to overcome the weaknesses of traditional improvement activities in addressing this type of loss. This book provides a disciplined step-by-step approach to identifying and eliminating causes of chronic equipment-related loss, thorough discussion with good illustrations, and case studies of implementation.
1-56327-035-8/ est. 200 pages / $85.00 / Order PMA-220

Eliminating Minor Stoppages on Automated Lines
Kikuo Suehiro

Stoppages of automated equipment lines severely affect productivity, cost, and lead time. Such losses make decreasing the number of stoppages a crucial element of TPM. Kikuo Suehiro has helped companies such as Hitachi achieve unprecedented reduction in the number of minor stoppages. In this explicitly detailed book, he presents a scientific approach to determining the causes of stoppages and the actions that can be taken to diminish their occurrence.
ISBN 1-56327-70-4 / 208 pages / $50.00 / Order ELIM-B220

New Directions for TPM
Tokutaro Suzuki

This is the first book to examine the multitude of possibilities for TPM (Total Productive Maintenance) beyond the realm of repetitive manufacturing. Suzuki, Vice Chairman of the Japan Institute of Plant Maintenance, examines four major shifts in the direction of TPM application:
- The increasingly effective use of TPM in process industries
- The acceleration of TPM implementation in original equipment manufacturing
- The spread of TPM to departments other than production and maintenance, including administration, research and development, and sales
- The proliferation of TPM activities in companies outside Japan
ISBN 1-56327-011-0 / 303 pages / $60.00 / Order NDTPM-B220

PRODUCTIVITY PRESS, INC., DEPT. BK, P.O. BOX 13390, PORTLAND, OR 97213-0390
Telephone: 1-800-394-6868   Fax: 1-800-394-6286

Introduction to TPM
Total Productive Maintenance
Seiichi Nakajima

Total Productive Maintenance (TPM) combines preventive maintenance with Japanese concepts of total quality control (TQC) and total employee involvement (TEI). The result is a new system for equipment maintenance that optimizes effectiveness, eliminates breakdowns, and promotes autonomous operator maintenance through day-to-day activities. Here are the steps involved in TPM and case examples from top Japanese plants.
ISBN 0-915299-23-2 / 149 pages / $45.00 / Order ITPM-B220

Equipment Planning for TPM
Maintenance Prevention Design
Fumio Gotoh

This practical book for design engineers, maintenance technicians, and manufacturing managers details a systematic approach to the improvement of equipment development and design and product manufacturing. The author analyzes five basic conditions for factory equipment of the future: development, reliability, economics, availability, and maintainability. The book's revolutionary concepts of equipment design and development enables managers to reduce equipment development time, balance maintenance and equipment planning and improvement, and improve quality production equipment.
ISBN 0-915299-77-1 / 337 pages / $85.00 / Order ETPM-B220

Quality Maintenance
Zero Defects Through Equipment Management
Seiji Tsuchiya

What must your company do to achieve zero-defect product quality? With the appropriate integration of advanced manufacturing techniques, you can trace defects to their root causes—and permanently eliminate them. In this practical book, Seiji Tsuchiya uses clear descriptions and specific examples to show managers and supervisors how to management equipment to produce higher quality goods. Learn how to apply the ideas and procedures of TPM to quality.
ISBN 0-915299-04-6 / 223 pages / $60.00 / Order QMAINT-B220

PRODUCTIVITY PRESS, INC., DEPT. BK, P.O. BOX 13390, PORTLAND, OR 97213-0390
Telephone: 1-800-394-6868   Fax: 1-800-394-6286

TPM Development Program
Implementing Total Productive Maintenance
Seiichi Nakajima (ed.)

This book outlines a three-year program for systematic TPM development and implementation. It describes in detail the five principal developmental activities of TPM:

- Systematic elimination of the six big equipment related losses through small group activities
- Autonomous maintenance (by operators)
- Scheduled maintenance for the maintenance department
- Training in operation and maintenance skills
- Comprehensive equipment management from the design stage

Long considered the "bible" of TPM, this book provides critical guidance for anyone implementing TPM.
ISBN 0-915299-37-2 / 428 pages / $85.00 / Order DTPM-B220

TPM for America
What It Is and Why You Need It
Herbert R. Steinbacher and Norma L. Steinbacher

As much as 15-40 percent of manufacturing costs are attributable to maintenance. With a fully implemented TPM program, your company can eradicate all but a fraction of these costs. Co-written by an American TPM practitioner and an experienced educator, this book gives a convincing account of why American companies must adopt TPM if we are to successfully compete in world markets. Includes examples from leading American companies showing how TPM has changed them.
ISBN 1-56327-044-7 / 169 pages / $25.00 / Order TPMAM-B220

TPM for Operators
Compiled by Productivity Press
Kunio Shirose, Advisory Editor

TPM for Operators offers an overview of the basic features of TPM as well as the implementation process in an easy-to-follow presentation. It focuses on the important role of operators in maximizing equipment effectiveness. For the most cost-effective on-site education, every front-line worker in your operation should read this book. It's the best way to ensure companywide understanding of TPM.
ISBN 1-56327-016-1 / 96 pages / $17.00 paper / Order TPMOP-B220

PRODUCTIVITY PRESS, INC., DEPT. BK, P.O. BOX 13390, PORTLAND, OR 97213-0390
Telephone: 1-800-394-6868   Fax: 1-800-394-6286

TPM in Process Industries

Tokutaro Suzuki (ed.)

Process industries have a particularly urgent need for collaborative equipment management systems like TPM that can absolutely guarantee safe, stable operation. In *TPM in Process Industries*, top consultants from JIPM (Japan Institute of Plant Maintenance) document approaches to implementing TPM in process industries. They focus on the process environment and equipment issues such as process loss structure and calculation, autonomous maintenance, equipment and process improvement, and quality maintenance. Must reading for any manager in the process industry.
ISBN 1-56327-036-6 / 400 pages / $85.00 / Order TPMPI-B220

Training for TPM
A Manufacturing Success Story

Nachi-Fujikoshi (ed.)

A detailed case study of TPM implementation at a world-class manufacturer of bearings, precision machine tools, dies, industrial equipment, and robots. In just 2-1/2 years the company was awarded Japan's prestigious PM Prize for its program. Here's a detailed account of their improvement activities—and an impressive model for yours.
ISBN 0-915299-34-8 / 274 pages / $65.00 / Order CTPM-B220

TO ORDER: Write, phone, or fax Productivity Press, Dept. BK, P.O. Box 13390, Portland, OR 97213-0390, phone 1-800-394-6868, fax 1-800-394-6286. Send check or charge to your credit card (American Express, Visa, MasterCard accepted).

U.S. ORDERS: Add $5 shipping for first book, $2 each additional for UPS surface delivery. Add $5 for each AV program containing 1 or 2 tapes; add $12 for each AV program containing 3 or more tapes. We offer attractive quantity discounts for bulk purchases of individual titles; call for more information.

INTERNATIONAL ORDERS: Write, phone, or fax for quote and indicate shipping method desired. For international callers, telephone number is 503-235-0600 and fax number is 503-235-0909. Prepayment in U.S. dollars must accompany your order (checks must be drawn on U.S. banks). When quote is returned with payment, your order will be shipped promptly by the method requested.

NOTE: Prices are in U.S. dollars and are subject to change without notice.